I Fought Like a *Girl,* and I Won!

5/28/2015

Kristen,
 Thank-you for your support & being friendly 😊. Your children are all well mannered! God Bless you & your family!
 All my Best
 Nicole Alyse Dorman

I Fought Like a *Girl,* and I Won!

Nicole Alyse Dorman

Copyright © 2015 by Nicole Alyse Dorman.

Library of Congress Control Number:	2015903776
ISBN: Hardcover	978-1-5035-5147-3
Softcover	978-1-5035-5149-7
eBook	978-1-5035-5148-0

All rights reserved. No part of this book may be reproduced or transmitted in any form or by any means, electronic or mechanical, including photocopying, recording, or by any information storage and retrieval system, without permission in writing from the copyright owner.

Any people depicted in stock imagery provided by Thinkstock are models, and such images are being used for illustrative purposes only.
Certain stock imagery © Thinkstock.

Print information available on the last page.

Rev. date: 03/20/2015

To order additional copies of this book, contact:
Xlibris
1-888-795-4274
www.Xlibris.com
Orders@Xlibris.com

CONTENTS

Preface ix

Chapter 1 Who Am I? 1
Chapter 2 Concerned About My Selfie! (My Self-Exam, Not My iPhone Selfie!) 5
Chapter 3 New Year, New Diagnosis 12
Chapter 4 The Game Plan: Tackling Breast Cancer 16
Chapter 5 Meeting My Medical Team 23
Chapter 6 Back to Work, or Is It? 31
Chapter 7 Breast Cancer Vocabulary 39
Chapter 8 I've Got Some Mail! I'm Sharing Some Cards and Letters from My Family, Friends, and Coworkers! 51
Chapter 9 Raising Breast Cancer Awareness Every Day! Telling My Story to Encourage Women (Especially Women Under Forty) to Get Yearly Mammograms! 65
Chapter 10 Eye of the Tiger! (My Facebook Diary My Mother Created for Me) 69
Chapter 11 Breast Cancer Resources 89

In loving memory of my grandmother, Pauline Joyce Adams Baker, 8/25/1926–10/22/1974. She was forty-eight years old when she lost her battle with breast cancer. I never had the chance to meet you, but I love you and miss you so much! RIP.

Thank you to my mother, Pamela, and stepfather, Wil, and my remaining family and extended family members for your support, love, and understanding!

Last but definitely not least, thank you to the staff/coworkers and parent friends at Mountain View Elementary School in Harker Heights, Texas. A million thank-yous cannot express my gratitude to all of you for being so supportive to my three children and me throughout my breast cancer journey!

Preface

I Fought Like a Girl, and I Won! is about my breast cancer journey from October 2013 until now. This is my first book, and I give it an *E* for everyone rating. Any cancer diagnosis, especially breast cancer, affects everyone from children through adults.

I'm a single mother of three kids with a monthly income of $1,100. My income includes my part-time income with the Killeen Independent School District. I also am receiving child support for only one child. A huge curve ball was thrown at me when I received a phone call from my doctor telling me of my core-needle biopsy results. My doctor told me I had invasive ductal carcinoma, a form of breast cancer!

My story reveals how I dealt with being told I was a statistic! The only difference was that I wasn't going down without a fight to survive! I discuss and educate readers about what I've endured throughout my journey. I share with readers how I told people about my diagnosis and how astonished I was for having so much love and support. I discuss and educate about my mastectomy and port-a-cath surgeries. I cut my hair very short before beginning chemotherapy in March 2014 to avoid it coming out in clumps.

My coworkers, parents, and friends at Mountain View Elementary were very envious (and still are) of me for returning to work with a smile on my face after every chemotherapy and radiation treatments. When I was asked how I could keep smiling after everything I had been through, I simply replied that I was happy and grateful for having a second chance in life. I was blessed to be able to come to work after chemotherapy; most people have no energy and want to stay in bed to recover.

Any cancer diagnosis doesn't put life on hold. Monthly bills are still going to come in like clockwork. Children still need to go to school and be cared for. I put everything in perspective once I was diagnosed. I didn't sweat the small things in life! Once I was diagnosed, I became a survivor! I am sharing all my experience that I had with breast cancer to educate, to spread awareness, and to save someone else's life!

My book contains my entire journey, references, and the organizations that have assisted me with grants. While I'm constantly being told that I'm inspiring too many people, I inspired myself to write this book! Everyone deserves a second chance in life; here is mine, and I'm going to shine!

Anastazija
Bingham

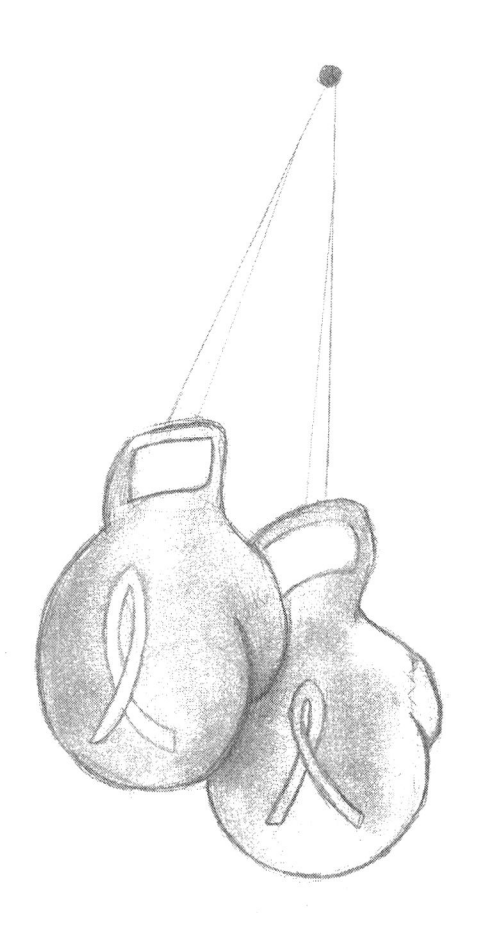

11/27/2014

1

Who Am I?

Let me introduce myself before I begin my story. I'm Nicole Alyse Dorman, born on January 15, 1979. I'm a single parent to three children—two boys, seven and nine, and a girl, fifteen. I was born in Philadelphia, Pennsylvania. I attended the Milton Hershey School in Hershey, Pennsylvania, from January 1989 to June 2, 1996. I enlisted in the US Army on June 7, 1996. I had eight weeks of basic training and eight weeks of advanced individual training (AIT) to attend cooking school. I was in the army reserves for a year while I attended East Stroudsburg University in East Stroudsburg, Pennsylvania. I majored in Spanish education; I wanted to become a Spanish teacher.

In May 1997, at the end of my first semester at ESU, I made the decision to join the army full time and to be on active duty. College life at ESU wasn't working out for me. I was fortunate to get orders for Dexheim, Germany. I enjoyed my three-year tour and did a lot of traveling when time allowed. I have been to Austria, Poland, Paris, Holland, and London. I have always enjoyed traveling, learning about different cultures and lifestyles of people. I have been living in Killeen, Texas, since February 2001. I had relocated to Killeen from Germany. I'm an honorably discharged army veteran and am grateful for the awesome medical care I have received at the Temple VA Hospital. Cancer is a very expensive illness; I don't know what I would have done if I didn't have medical coverage through the VA. I currently am a crossing guard for the Killeen Independent School District (KISD). It is a part-time position where I work twenty hours a week. I love my job and wouldn't trade it for the world!

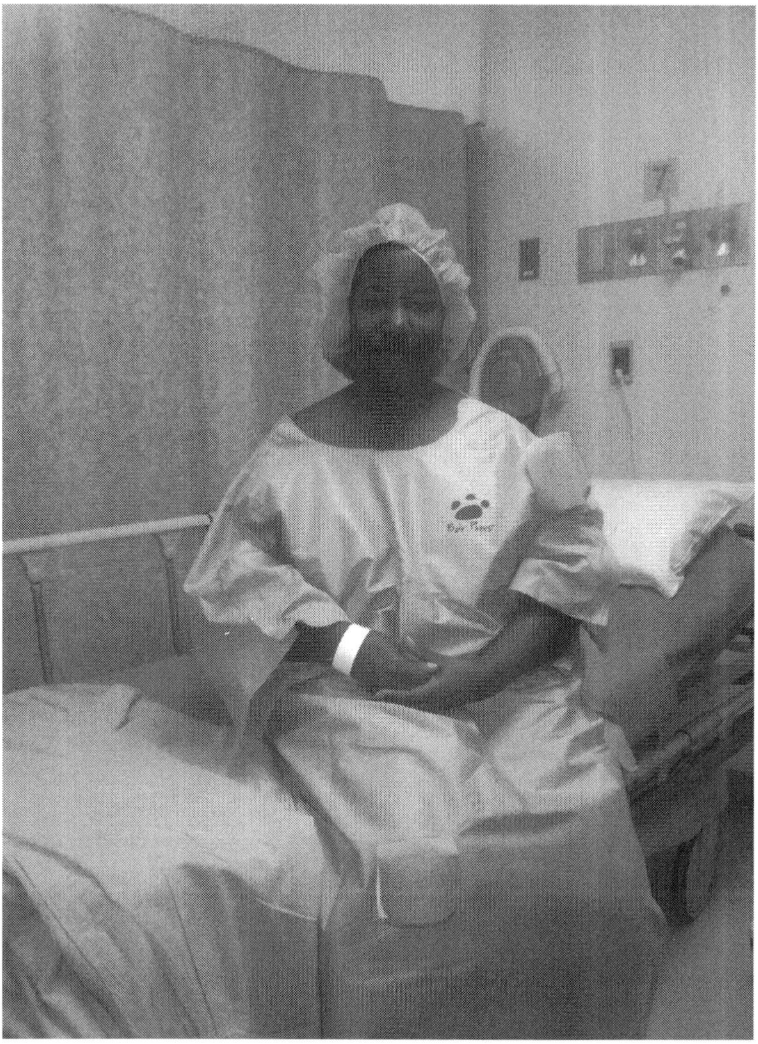

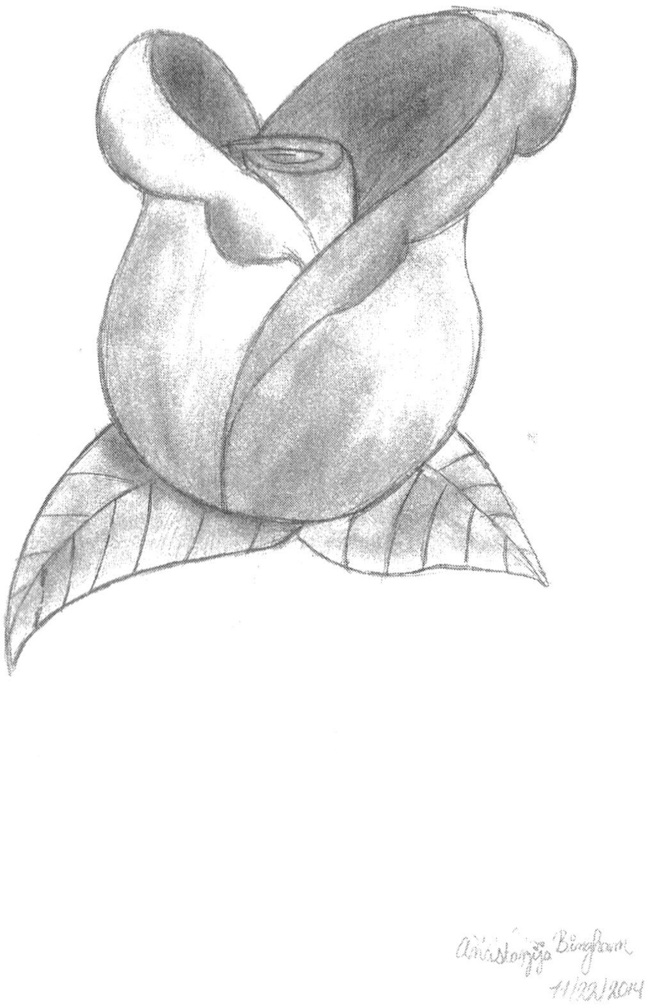

2

Concerned About My Selfie! (My Self-Exam, Not My iPhone Selfie!)

In the middle of October 2013, I detected a painful lump in my right breast. I didn't think much of it, but I wanted to get it looked at. I called the Women's Clinic at the Temple VA Hospital to make an appointment. The clerk on the phone whom I spoke with told me I could come in as soon as possible to do a walk-in mammogram. I was able to get a ride from a close friend of mine to the Women's Clinic on Wednesday, November 27, 2013. When I went to check in with my veterans ID card, I was told there were no walk-in mammograms! I explained to the clerk that I was told over the phone that I could come and do a walk-in and be seen today! There was no way I was going to go home without any answers! I had to be persistent but in a fashionable manner. My last plea to be seen was telling the clerk that my friend had taken time off from work to give me and my children a ride to Temple, Texas, from Killeen, Texas (forty-minute drive).

Moments later, a female nurse called me back to a room and asked me what my concern was. I told the nurse that I had complaints of a painful lump on my right breast that hurt all the time. I had a physical exam of both breasts, and there was no doubt that the right breast was significantly swollen! The nurse asked me what my pain level was; I wanted to say one hundred, but I could only go as high as ten! The nurse told me that the lump was a "possible cyst." I didn't think the lump was a cyst because I didn't feel any fluid in it, only a hard mass.

Obviously, I'm not a doctor, but I know my own body when something isn't right. The nurse said there was no reason to do a mammogram on me because I wasn't forty! Apparently, the fact that breast cancer is hereditary in my family didn't raise any red flags! My walk-in appointment was concluded by the nurse advising me to pick up a heating pad from the prosthetic department upstairs. The heat from the heating pad would alleviate the pain and discomfort I was having. I was also prescribed naproxen 500 mg for pain and amoxicillin just in case the "possible cyst" was some kind of infection. The nurse put in an order for an ultrasound to be done on me.

The next two and a half weeks went by as normal. I kept busy with work and taking care of my children. I was taking the naproxen and amoxicillin as prescribed and also applying the heating pad throughout the day. The "possible cyst" was getting bigger and more painful!

It was the first week of December 2013 when I received a phone call from the Temple VA Women's Clinic. I finally had an appointment for December 18, 2013, for the ultrasound appointment! Unfortunately, I wasn't able to make that appointment, but I called to reschedule for a January 2, 2014, appointment. Christmas and New Year 2014 went by faster than I could bat my eyelashes!

At my appointment, I was extremely scared and worried, and I had some anxiety about the ultrasound being done. I remember that I was talking along and being inquisitive! Who wouldn't be when there is a procedure being done on them? My eyes kept shifting from the screen to the technologist's face. She looked very concerned, and I could tell something was wrong. I had asked her if everything was okay. She responded by saying, "The doctor will talk to you in a few minutes. He'll go over the results with you." I thanked her and waited a few minutes for the doctor, but it seemed more like an hour!

The doctor came in and introduced himself. He explained that the lump wasn't a cyst but something difficult to diagnose at that time. I also found out that I had a lot of calcification underneath my right breast. Calcification is the accumulation of calcium salts in a body tissue. It has nothing to do with the amount of calcium in your body! The doctor told me I was going to need to have a mammogram done and a core-needle biopsy. The doctor asked me if I would be able to return on January 3, 2014, for the procedure. I told him that I wouldn't be able to return and asked if the biopsy could be done while I was already there at the Women's Clinic.

I had the core-needle biopsy performed on January 2, 2014, right after I had the bilateral (both breasts) mammogram done. The mammogram wasn't too bad; it was just painful because the lump on my right breast was being squished down! Ladies who have had mammograms done know what I'm talking about! =)

The core-needle biopsy, on the other hand, was very painful! I'm the type of person who doesn't flinch at the sight of a needle; however, having a long, hollow needle entering a sensitive area was very unpleasant for me! This special needle had a trigger at the end of it to pull out breast tissue samples. When the doctor pulled the trigger, it also made a loud noise. Normally, two to three samples are collected, but the doctor took six samples to be on the safe side. He didn't want me to have to come back to have another biopsy done if the samples weren't good enough. I had a liquid metal marker injected in my right breast so that when I had future mammograms, the doctor would know that I had tissue removed. Once the tissue samples were in the specimen cup, I was allowed to see them; after all, I was so involved with the procedure, asking every question in the book as to what was going on and what was happening next. The samples looked like silkworms in a clear liquid. The nurse told me that I would have my biopsy results in about five days. She gave me my brief aftercare instructions:

- * No strenuous activities for a few days.
- * Take naproxen 500 mg for pain as needed.
- * Put the reusable gel pack in the freezer for cold compresses or in the microwave for hot compresses to help with the swelling.
- * Most importantly, get plenty of rest. (Being a single mother of three kids gives me no time for any extra rest [LOL].)

I had returned home around 4:00 p.m., and at 6:00 p.m., my two boys, my friend, and I were on our way to the Austin-Bergstrom Airport to pick up my daughter from spending the holidays with her dad. It was hard to tell my children that they couldn't give me a big hug and that Mommy was in a lot of pain. When they asked why I was in pain, I could only tell them that I had a procedure done and that I had to take it easy for a few days to heal. I continued to pray about my biopsy results, hoping for the best. I was expecting a phone call sometime on January 7, 2014, with my results.

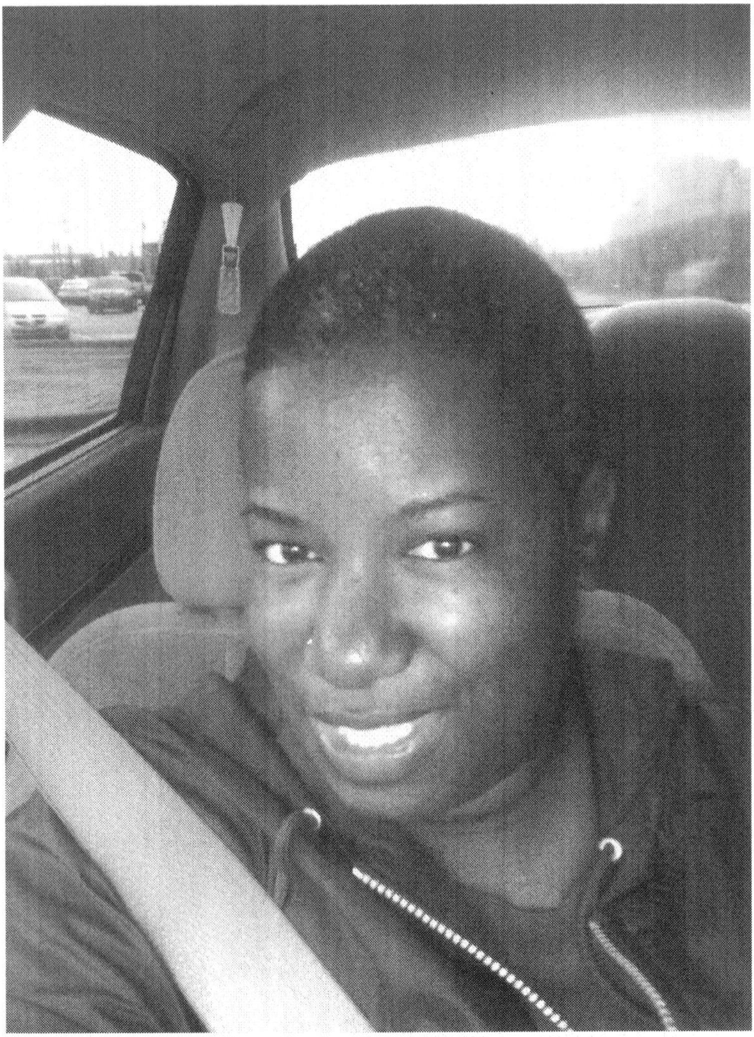

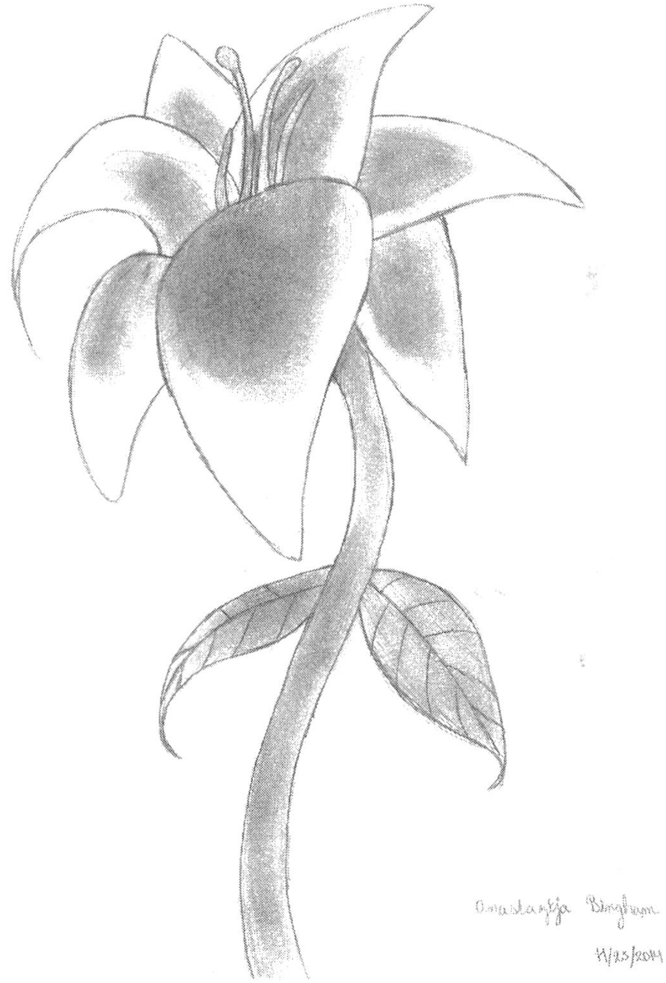

3

New Year, New Diagnosis

Tuesday, January 7, 2014, had finally arrived. I had nervously called the VA Women's Clinic at noon to find out if my biopsy results were in. There were no results. At 3:00 p.m., the nurse who originally saw me and did the visual exam in November 2013 had called me to tell me my results.

This was the phone call that would change my life forever. She nonchalantly said, "You have invasive ductal carcinoma." I asked her to repeat what she said; I mean, I heard her. I just wanted to hear the medical term again. I didn't know what the medical terminology meant. The nurse repeated, "You have invasive ductal carcinoma, a form of breast cancer!"

Right then and there, I just learned two things: (1) I had just been diagnosed with breast cancer, and (2) there was more than one form of breast cancer! At that very moment, my heart skipped a beat. I was in shock, and I started to feel sick to my stomach after hearing those two words: *breast cancer*! The nurse said that the good news was that breast cancer has a 95 percent survival rate if diagnosed early. Being diagnosed with breast cancer was definitely not on my list of New Year's resolutions! In the back of my mind, I was hoping that my results were a medical mix-up. (Hey, these things happen all the time!) Wait! I remembered that at the beginning of the phone call, I had to verify my name and social security number. I was still at work, on a break. I had to regain my composure to finish up my day before I could let the news sink in.

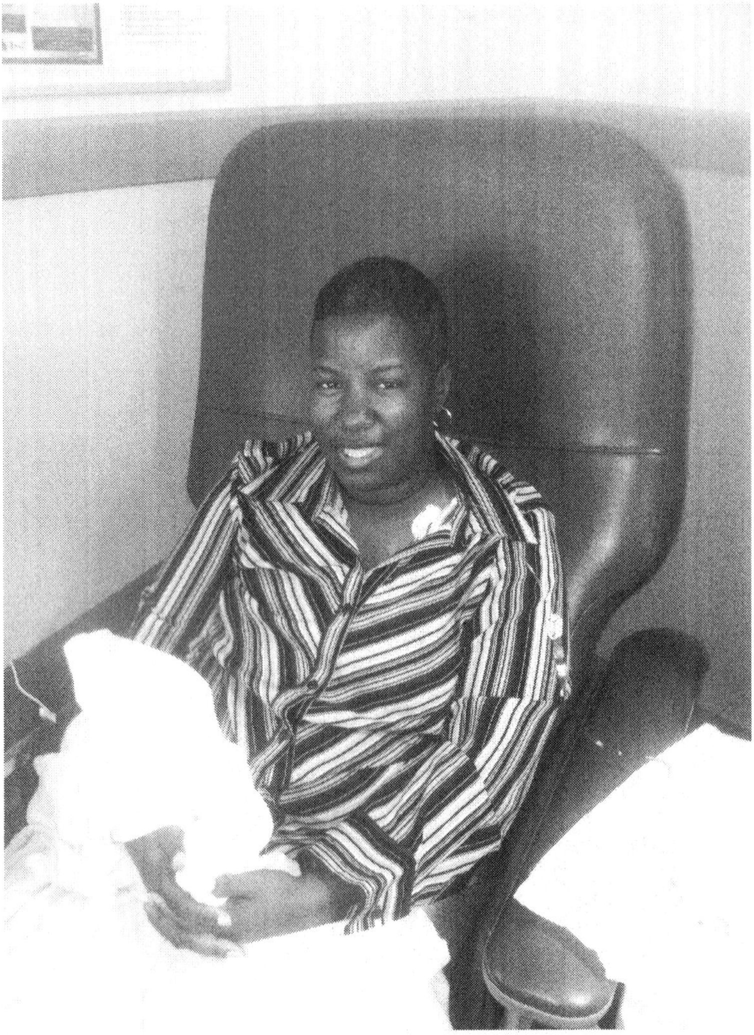

Anastazja Bingham
11/23/2014

4

The Game Plan: Tackling Breast Cancer

The nurse said that I would be working with a team of specialists and that I would have to make some crucial decisions. My VA medical team included my primary care doctor, oncologist, and surgeon. The nurse explained that I would definitely have to have surgery to get rid of most of the cancer. The surgery would be either a lumpectomy or a mastectomy, and my consultation with the surgeon would give me a better understanding of what would be better for me in my situation. The nurse concluded the phone conversation by saying, "Don't hesitate to call me in the next few days if you have any questions."

I had a million questions... I was scared, and even worse, I was thinking about how I was going to tell people about my new diagnosis. Any cancer diagnosis is not an easy subject to discuss. The news can, and will, affect everyone differently. I had my list of people whom I wanted and needed to tell, but I wasn't sure about how to go about doing it. I have no problem talking to people and being a social butterfly, but this was a brand-new ball game! When you tell people you're diagnosed with breast cancer (or any other serious illness), you receive a more dramatic response, and you might have to repeat what you just announced!

I decided to call my mother in Pennsylvania first. I was on a break at work and wanted to tell her and my stepfather, Wil, before I picked up my children from school. I was hoping to get their voice mail and leave a quick message saying, "Hi, Mom and Wil, call me back when you have a moment to talk, I love you!"

Scratch that thought; my mom answered, and I had to let her know I had just received my biopsy results. I asked her if she was sitting down (parents, you automatically know that when your child, or children, ask you if you're sitting down, it's *big news*!); she said that she was. There was no beating around the bush; I told my mom straight-out that I was diagnosed with invasive ductal carcinoma, a form of breast cancer. I informed her that I would be seeing my primary care doctor, an oncologist, a surgeon, and possibly other medical doctors. I told my mom that I would be updating her and Wil with news about my future appointments and updates as I received them. My phone conversation with my mom lasted roughly about five to seven minutes. I had to get back to work, but I also knew that she didn't want to stay on the phone too long with me. When I told my mom the news, I think she may have had flashbacks to when she was fourteen, in 1972, and her mother (my maternal grandmother) was diagnosed with breast cancer. I hadn't begun to play out in my mind how I was going to break the news to my children.

I spent a lot of time on the Internet, researching invasive ductal carcinoma (IDC) and calcification. I found out that invasive ductal carcinoma starts in your breast ducts (no-brainer there) and that 75 to 80 percent of women have this type of breast cancer. Men can get breast cancer too; it's just not as common! The cancer can spread to other vital organs if not treated in time! I was getting worried because the only information I knew was that I had IDC. I didn't know how long I had this cancer in my body, what stage I was in, or how big the tumor was! I didn't know if I was going to live another year or not. I was beginning to feel overwhelmed, but I needed to calm down. I would soon find out the answers to all my questions.

I contacted the American Cancer Society for support, and they sent me a "Welcome to Breast Cancer!" packet. The packet had a wealth of knowledge and explained different services that the American Cancer Society offered. It was nice that they offered rides to my oncologist appointments at the Temple VA. I only used their pickup service twice, but the volunteers that I had were really nice.

I had originally planned on waiting until I met my oncologist to sit down with my children and have "the talk." I had read a section on the American Cancer Society on how to tell your children you have cancer.

The site was extremely helpful and gave me guidance on how to tell my then six-, eight-, and fourteen-year-old children that I was sick. I didn't want to overwhelm them with information that they wouldn't fully understand. I called my children in the den for a family meeting. There are some things in life in which there are no right or wrong way to go about doing. I looked in my children's eyes and said, "There's no easy way to say this, but Mommy has breast cancer."

My daughter, who was fourteen years old at the time, had a better understanding of what I had just said. She took the news the hardest and ran out of the room, crying and screaming, "Say it isn't true!" I told her to come back in the den because running away wasn't going to make the cancer automatically disappear. I hugged all my kids tightly and told them that I love them so much. I explained that they cannot catch cancer from me and that breast cancer wasn't a death sentence for me. I told them that my appearance was going to change, and I would need them to help more around the house. I told my kids that I would lose my hair when I had to do chemotherapy treatments; I might lose some weight, be more tired than usual. There is a long laundry list of breast cancer side effects, but I wanted to give them the short list and not scare them. I kept calm and remained strong while talking to them. I knew that if I broke down in tears while talking, my kids would cry too! Overall, the discussion went better than I expected it to.

I found out a lot about my newly diagnosed illness:

1. A cancer diagnosis puts everything in a new perspective!

2. A cancer diagnosis doesn't stop the bills from coming in!

3. A cancer diagnosis lets you know who is really there for you!

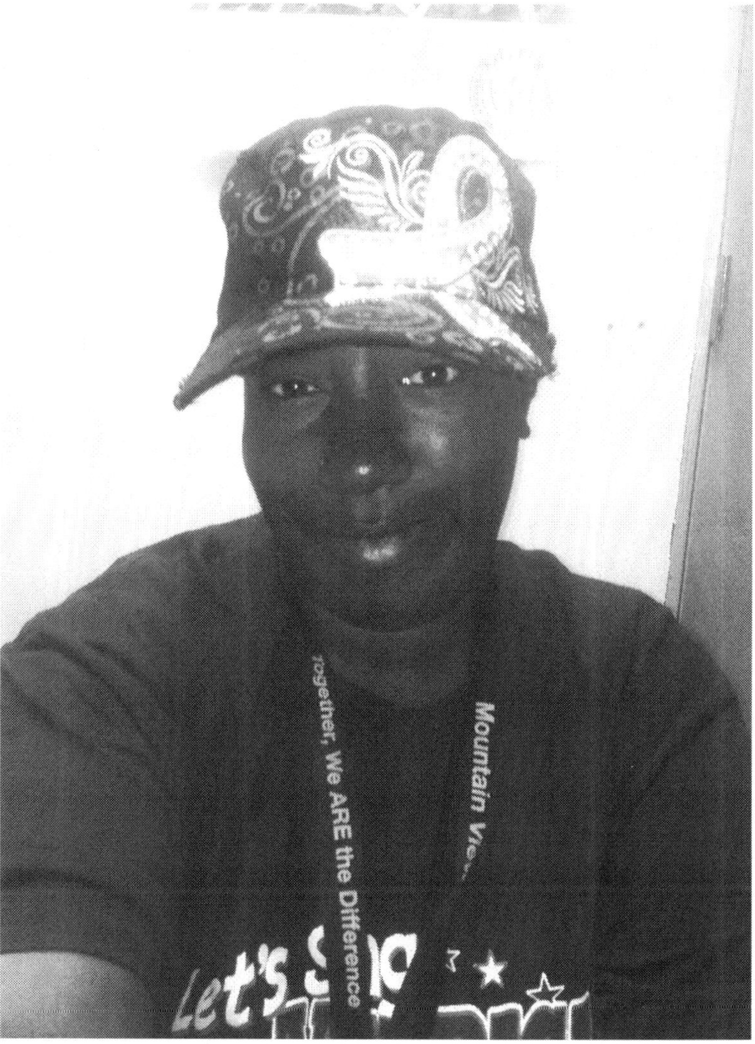
We ARE the Difference
Mountain

Anastazija Bingham
11/26/2014

5

Meeting My Medical Team

January 14, 2014, I had an appointment to meet my oncologist. I received more information and got the opportunity to ask some questions that have been swarming in my mind for a week. I must have had a thousand questions! When it comes to your health, there are no limits of how many questions you can ask. No one can rush you when you have an appointment either.

As soon as introductions were made, my oncologist told me that I had to have a mastectomy. The size of my tumor and the amount of calcification underneath were too much to try to save. If I had a lumpectomy to get rid of the tumor, in time, the calcification would have turned into cancer cells. I didn't want that, and I agreed to have the mastectomy performed. I asked my oncologist what stage and grade my cancer was. She explained that information was unknown until I had surgery and a pathology report was completed. Every cancer journey is different; some women can have chemotherapy treatments to shrink the tumor down and then have a lumpectomy, followed by radiation treatments. For me, my journey would start with a mastectomy, followed by chemotherapy and possible radiation. Breast reconstruction would be delayed for six months to one year after my mastectomy. You know what? I was determined to do everything I could do in order to be here for my children and loved ones!

January 15, 2014, was my thirty-fifth birthday. It was a great day overall. I was doing "awesome" (no lie) for a woman who received a breast cancer diagnosis a week prior! I had begun to inform my coworkers at Mountain View Elementary about my health. Every time I told someone the news, it really dawned on me that I really did have cancer. Reality finally hit me! I wasn't in denial that I was sick. I still felt healthy and my normal self. I have never smoked cigarettes, and I drink in moderation, so what gives?

On January 17, 2014, I had a consultation with the surgeon who was going to perform my mastectomy. I was the question queen again! This time, I asked the anesthesiologist a lot of questions since I had no previous surgeries. I had never been put to sleep, and I wanted to make sure that I was going to be calm for the big procedure. I had put everything in God's hands and prayed on my situation!

My surgeon had set a January 28, 2014, date. I only had eleven days to prepare myself and make arrangements for my children because I was going to be in the hospital overnight. I needed to have someone pick me up once I was discharged from the hospital. I had many appointments to go to before my surgery to make sure my body was healthy and strong enough to have the mastectomy. I had done a CAT scan, EKG, blood work, to name a few things. I also had blood drawn for the BRCA1 test to see if I carried the breast cancer gene. It took four weeks to get the results of that test; fortunately, I am *not* a carrier! Many thanks go out to my good friend (she knows who she is) for picking me up and helping me out a lot! ☺

January 27, 2014, I had a visit from a coworker (assistant principal), Mrs. T. She had come to the house, leaving food, drinks, and snacks for the kids and me. Mrs. T told me that a bunch of coworkers at Mountain View Elementary had donated money to purchase enough food for the next month. It was really nice that my coworkers have done that because it made things a little easier for me to recover from the surgery.

January 28, 2014, was here! There was no turning back; it literally was a do-or-die situation! My good friend took me to the Temple VA at 9:00 a.m. My surgery time was scheduled for 11:00 a.m. I had checked in, was explained the process of getting changed into my "gear," and was waiting in the waiting area, and I was nervous as hell! I was handed a blue buzzer (the kind you get when you're waiting for your table at a restaurant). When the buzzer started blinking, it was time for me to go back and get ready for showtime!

The surgery was a success, and I had come into the recovery area at 3:30 p.m. My friend who had driven me to the VA was extremely worried about me because no one had given her an update about me. My cousin Joyce, who lives in the Austin area, had come to visit me once I was assigned a room upstairs. I hadn't seen my cousin since March 2010, so I was glad to see her briefly. Joyce had told me that my breast cancer diagnosis was a wake-up call for her to start getting yearly mammograms and to keep in touch more often with family.

I really had my mind set on going home the evening of my surgery, but I was told that I had to stay overnight for observations. Who was I kidding? I did just have a major surgery! I was in a lot less pain than I had anticipated; morphine works wonders! ☺

It was difficult for me to look in the mirror and look at my new battle scar. I had mixed emotions on how my life was going to be with my new image. I shouldn't have; after all, I was alive! I was thinking about some what-if questions: "What if I looked like a freak to other people?" and "What if I felt like I was less of a woman because of having the mastectomy?" I was even worried about how I would be treated when I would return to work. I know that everyone knew my situation and what I had just been through, but I was so worried about a lot of things. None of that should have mattered because I was determined to be a survivor!

I was discharged from the Temple VA Hospital on January 29, 2014, and I was off work for four weeks. I was in pain for about two and a half weeks. I had five lymph nodes removed (axillary dissection) during the mastectomy, and the lymph nodes were tested to determine what stage I was in. It would take another four weeks to get my pathology report to find out the answer. I had to have two Jackson-Pratt drains (JP drains) in my right side to drain fluids from my mastectomy.

The drains were bigger than the drawings I had seen online; they looked like plastic grenades! I was instructed on how to empty them out and to create a vacuum so that the tubes could pull out the excess fluids. It was quite easy, and luckily, I do not get squeamish at the sight of blood. The only thing I didn't like about the drains is that they were stitched into my side for ten days! I felt like a marionette puppet with limited mobility!

My discharge nurse advised me to get plenty of rest. Ha! That was not going to be easy, especially with three children. There was housework that needed to be done, laundry, etc. Life doesn't stop when you're diagnosed with breast cancer! I did get some rest in the mornings, but afternoons, I did laundry, vacuumed, swept, and mopped the floors. I didn't overdo anything because I was on an order of lifting no more than ten pounds for six weeks.

I wanted to exercise and use my right arm as much as possible. I am at risk for lymphedema for the rest of my life since I had the mastectomy. I just have to be careful to not cut my right hand or arm. I can wear a compression sleeve at night if I want. I can't have my blood pressure taken on my right arm anymore or any IVs taken from my right arm. I have to be careful with what I do; being at risk for lymphedema is a bit scary, but it doesn't limit me from doing anything!

When I was discharged from the Temple VA Hospital, I wasn't given any resources on where to seek any kind of assistance. I had to do my own research. I wasn't able to get a home health aide to help me at home because I wasn't old enough! If I had been a senior citizen who just had a mastectomy, then I would have qualified to have a nurse come to the house and help clean my surgery site, change bandages, etc. I'm in no way complaining; I am very grateful that I was able to get good medical treatment at the Temple VA.

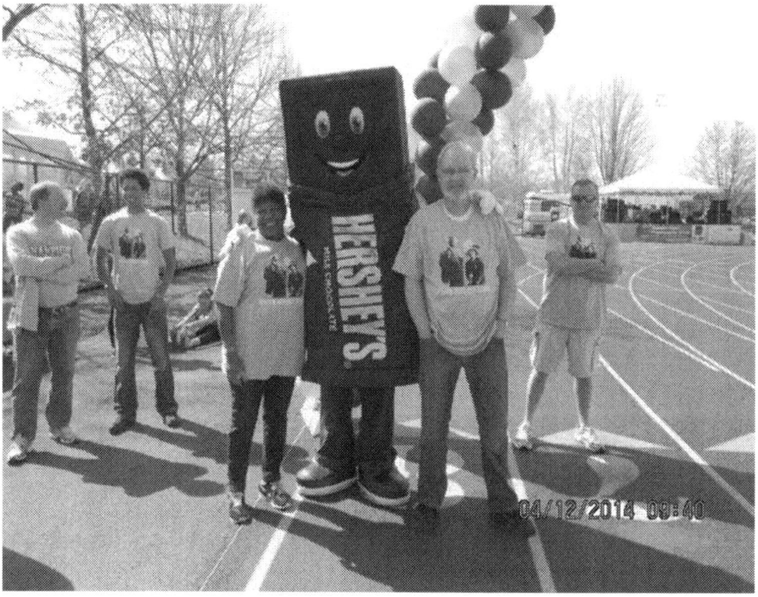
HERSHEY'S
04/12/2014 09:40

Anastazija Bingham
11/23/2004

6

Back to Work, or Is It?

The last week of February, I had called my boss to remind her that I was returning to work on March 3, 2014. She was glad to hear that I was healing well and was returning to work. I had also informed her that I would be starting chemotherapy sometime in March. When I told her that, she told me how she was just recently informed that part-time employees for KISD are not qualified for the Family Leave Medical Act (FMLA). My disposition immediately went from happy to concerned; suddenly, I wondered how undergoing chemotherapy treatments would affect me and my crossing-guard job. My boss reminded me that I had already used all my sick leave! I did have a lot of presurgery appointments that were during my work hours. This news flash meant that depending on how I felt after my chemotherapy treatments, I may be *fired* from my job if I didn't come to work. That wasn't what I was expecting to hear, but that's life! I had read that many chemotherapy patients are really tired after a treatment and are in bed for one to two days after treatment! Time would tell what was in store for me.

March 18, I had to have another surgery to have a medi-port put in my chest. I have small veins, and receiving chemotherapy every two weeks would have me bruised worse than a peach! The surgery is normally a twenty-minute procedure where the port and catheter tube are put in through your veins. My surgery went about an hour because of complications; I had to have the catheter fed through my jugular vein, which you can see sticking out of my neck. My neck and chest were painful for the first few days after surgery.

My chemotherapy began on March 19, 2014. I started with two medicines at the same time. I had Adriamycin (red) and Cytoxan (clear). Adriamycin is the most toxic chemotherapy drug out there, with the most side effects. I was in chemotherapy for two and a half to three hours. I had my appointments scheduled at 11:00 a.m., so I had a lunch tray in the chemotherapy room. I didn't feel sick until the next day after chemotherapy. I felt nauseous and fatigued, and two days after chemotherapy, I had to give myself a shot in the stomach. The shot is called Neulasta, and it helps to boost your white blood count. The Neulasta shot had to be refrigerated until I self-administered it in my stomach. I had horrible bone pain within twenty-four hours after giving myself the shot, and it really hurt! The allover bone pain lasted about two to three days. I took naproxen for pain. Remarkably, I always went to work the day after chemotherapy with a smile on my face! I count it a blessing that I was able to get out of bed to come to work. I had to; my job was on the line! It was not easy by a long shot, and I wasn't always feeling my best, but it was doable.

As soon as I would feel better, it was time for another chemotherapy treatment. I really didn't have time to rest and relax after my chemotherapy treatments. I had my children to take care of. In life, we all have to make sacrifices. I had breast cancer, but I wasn't going to use that as a crutch and be lazy. I also was not going to sit in a corner and feel bad for myself because I had this illness. I was going to stay positive and had my mind set to beat breast cancer! Every chemotherapy treatment, I had my blood drawn from my medi-port for my lab work. The labs were necessary for my oncologist to monitor my blood counts.

In April 2014, I was fitted for a mastectomy bra and a breast prosthesis. I was almost four months postsurgery, and I finally had a sense of balance. I felt normal and looked normal! I was very pleased with my prosthesis and bras.

Not everyone handles a breast cancer diagnosis the same, and not every experience is the same. It was easy for me to remain positive and hopeful that I was going to win the fight. I wanted to be another statistic—a survivor statistic! I had the attitude that I was going to beat breast cancer; I was determined that it wasn't my time to leave yet! You may not realize that when you smile at someone, you may make someone's day. A smile goes a long way; you never know until you smile at someone or receive a smile back.

July 30, 2014, through September 10, 2014, I underwent thirty treatments of radiation at the Killeen Cancer Center. I had the most awesome, upbeat, professional radiology staff I've ever met! I went to my appointments Monday to Friday at 9:30 a.m. I felt that radiation was a slice of pie, compared to the chemotherapy treatments I endured every two weeks for four months! I had very few side effects, which included fatigue, darkening of my skin at the treatment sites, and skin tenderness. The final two weeks of my radiation were the most painful for me. My skin had started to peel under my right armpit and around my mastectomy site. There was a foul odor (which I was told was normal), and I had swelling everywhere I was peeling. I had pain that wouldn't quit! I was prescribed pain medicine, which I only took at night so I could go to sleep. During the day, I tolerated the pain while I was at work. Even though I've completed all my radiation, my radiology oncologist wants to do follow-up appointments every few months with me to make sure my skin is healing properly.

I am fortunate that I detected my breast cancer early on! I had endured a lot through my journey, but my friends, family, faith, hope, courage, and positive attitude helped me win my battle. I have been taking tamoxifen since September. I have to take this pill once a day for five years. I will be having reconstruction surgery in the spring of 2015.

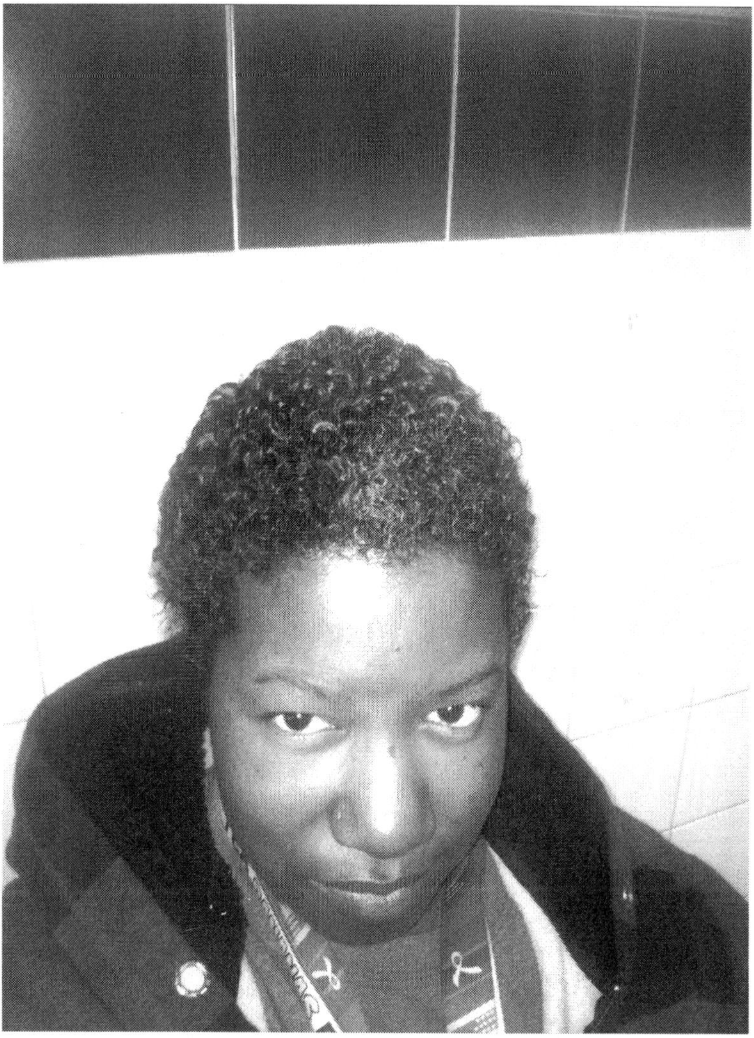

Anastasyja Bingham
12/6/2014

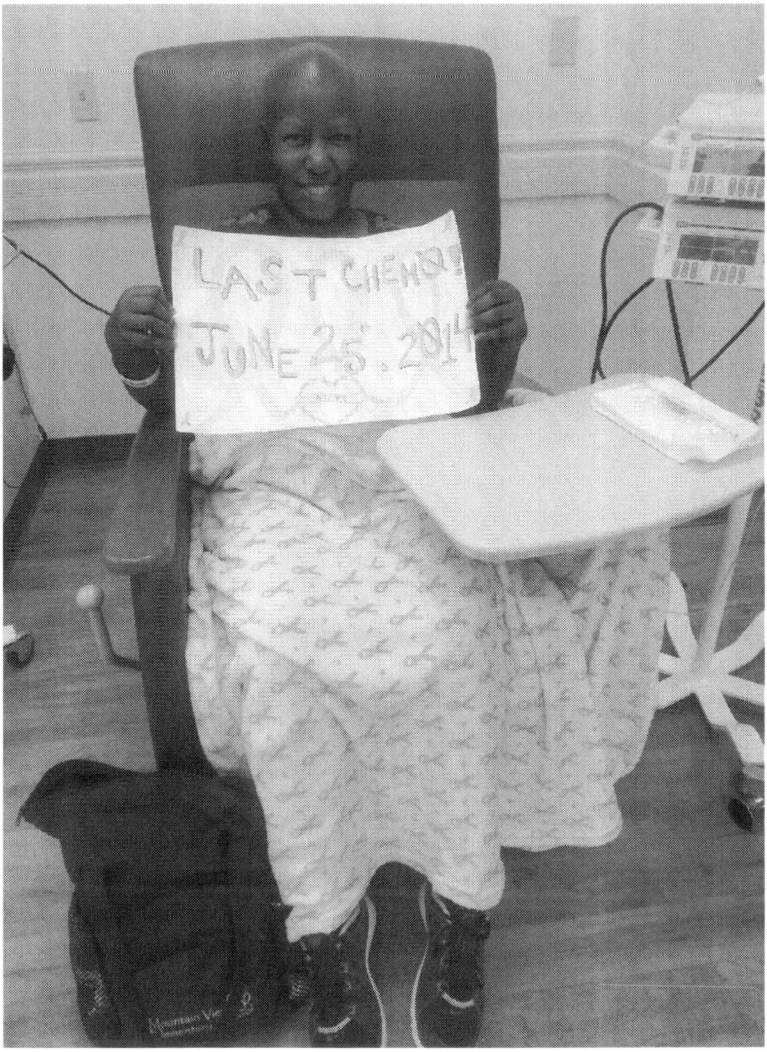
LAST CHEMO!
JUNE 25. 2014

Anastazija Bingham
11/26/2014

7

Breast Cancer Vocabulary

The following vocabulary words are everything that I went through during my journey and have yet to experience!

A

Adjuvant treatment—therapy offered in addition to an initial surgical procedure to decrease the risk of relapse.

Fact: I underwent chemotherapy and radiation, and currently I am going through hormonal therapy. I am prescribed 20 mg of tamoxifen daily for the next five years.

Alopecia—a condition that causes the loss of hair from anywhere on your body, mainly the scalp.

Fact: I cut my hair short before I started chemotherapy. I knew that the first two chemotherapy medicines I was about to take would cause hair loss. I didn't want my hair falling out in clumps! When my hair did fall out, my scalp was extremely tender and sore!

Analgesic—any drug that is prescribed or administered to take away pain without the loss of consciousness by blocking messages transferred between the brain and pain receptor sites.

Fact: Morphine is an analgesic. I had morphine administered through my IV after I had my right mastectomy. Hydrocodone is another analgesic. I was prescribed this and only took it at night because of the side effects, not to mention it is a narcotic! I had also taken hydrocodone when I was peeling and had painful radiation burns!

Antiemetic—a drug taken to alleviate nausea and vomiting.

Fact: I was prescribed medicine to help me avoid feeling nauseated after each chemotherapy round.

Axillary dissection (lymph node)—the surgical removal of lymph nodes located in the armpit area.

Fact: During my mastectomy, I had five lymph nodes removed. My biopsy results revealed that one out of five removed lymph nodes contained cancer cells.

B

Biopsy—the removal and microscopic analysis of a small piece of live tissues performed to determine an accurate diagnosis.

Fact: I had a needle core biopsy in December 2013, and the results told me that my cancer was 2.2 cm × 2.5 cm (2 in x 2.5 in).

Bone scan—a medical procedure that involves a radioactive substance (tracer) injected into a vein. The tracer travels from the bloodstream to the bones, allowing for a scanner to photograph the condition of the bones.

Fact: I had to do a bone scan in January 2014 before having the surgery.

BRCA1—a tumor suppressor gene embedded with the instructions to produce a protein that helps maintain a healthy cell division and growth as well as repair damaged DNA, if possible, and destroy it if unable to repair. BRCA1 derives its name from being the first discovered hereditary gene mutation associated with a higher risk of developing breast cancer.

Fact: I had blood drawn to be tested and sent to a lab to see if I carried the BRCA1 gene. Fortunately, the test results came back negative.

Breast cancer—the development of malignant (cancerous) cells that originate in the tissues of the breast, usually the duct and lobules.

Fact: I had invasive ductal carcinoma.

Breast implant—a prosthetic device consisting of a silicone outer shell and filled with a silicone gel or saline (salt water) that is implanted to augment, reconstruct, or create the physical form of female breasts.

Fact: One of my reconstruction options is to have a breast implant.

C

*Cance*r—term used to describe nearly 1—disease characterized by a malignant and invasive tumor caused by the uncontrolled division and growth of abnormal cells.

Fact: I had breast cancer!

Cancer cell—abnormal cell that divides and reproduces with uncontrolled growth, becoming part of a malignant tumor when conjoined with other like cells.

Fact: I had five lymph nodes that contained cancer cells.

Carcinoma—referring to any cancer that initially develops in the skin or other tissues, including breast tissue.

Fact: I had invasive ductal carcinoma.

CAT scan (computer axial tomography)/CT scan (computed tomography)—a cross-sectional image of the body produced by using x-ray technology that may include the liver, blood vessels, organs, or soft tissue.

Fact: I had to have a CT scan before I had my mastectomy in January 2014.

Chemotherapy—treatment of cancer that uses chemotherapeutic agents that are selectively destructive and toxic to malignant cells and tissue.

Fact: I had four months of chemotherapy. I took a total of three chemotherapy drugs—Adriamycin, Cytoxan, and Taxol. I went every two weeks for my treatments.

Chronic—used to describe a disease or health condition that has a long duration (more than three months) or recurs frequently.

Fact: My breast cancer lasted more than three months. I had found the lump in October 2013 but was diagnosed in January 2014.

Core biopsy—diagnostic medical procedure in which a thin, hollow needle is inserted into the lump or mass. The doctor may obtain a more accurate diagnosis by examining the tissue sample under a microscope.

Fact: I had a core-needle biopsy performed on January 2, 2014. I had six samples extracted from the tumor.

E

Estrogen—a group of compounds of hormones produced primarily by the ovaries that are responsible for menstrual cyclical changes and for the development and maintenance of secondary sex characteristics.

Estrogen receptor (ER)—refers to a protein receptor found within cells that, once activated by the hormone estrogen, allows the estrogen to bind to DNA, which may cause the cell to grow. Fact: My breast cancer was caused by estrogen receptors.

HER2/neu (human epidermal growth factor receptor 2)—refers to a gene that is responsible for sending signals to the cells with instructions to divide, grow, or repair. A mutation (HER2-positive) only occurs in certain cancer cells, which promotes the division and growth of the cells. A HER2 mutation is not hereditary. Fifteen to 20 percent of all breast cancers are HER2/neu-positive.

I

Invasive carcinoma—refers to cancer cells that penetrate the basement membrane, which allows the cells to invade or spread to the surrounding healthy tissue.

L

Lymphedema—refers to localized fluid retention or swelling (usually in an arm or a leg) due to an obstruction in the lymphatic system; damage to or removal of lymph nodes can cause lymphedema.

Fact: I'm at risk for lymphedema in my right arm due to having five lymph nodes removed. I can't have any blood draws or blood pressure taken on my right arm. I also have to be careful to not cut my right hand or right arm.

Lymph nodes—round- or oval-shaped structures distributed throughout the body, including the armpits and stomach. These structures act as filters for harmful substances and contain cells that attack germs and help fight infection.

Fact: I had five lymph nodes removed when I had my mastectomy. My pathology report found that the breast cancer was trying to spread to other organs in my body.

M

Malignant tumor—a cancerous mass of tissue that has no physiological purpose other than to survive and grow.

Fact: I had a malignant tumor that I detected on my right breast in October 2013. I grew more concerned when the tumor got bigger!

Mammogram—refers to a medical procedure that produces an x-ray image of the breast. Mammograms are used by doctors to detect any abnormalities such as tumors.

Fact: My doctor refused to give me a mammogram in November 2013 because I wasn't forty! I asked for another opinion, especially since I have a family history of breast cancer.

Mastectomy—the surgical removal of all or part of one or both breasts.

Fact: I had a simple mastectomy where all the tissue, breast, and nipple were removed! That was my first surgery, and it was considered major surgery and was pretty scary! I came through with flying colors!

O

Oncologist—a doctor who specializes in the diagnosis, study, and treatment of neoplastic diseases, particularly cancer.

Fact: My oncologist is very a understanding and patient doctor (no pun intended)! My first meeting with her was on January 14, 2014. Although I'm in remission now, I still see her every month, and I have to do labs through my medi-port.

P

Pathology—the scientific study of the nature of diseases, with an emphasis on the structural and functional changes in bodily tissue as a disease progresses.

Fact: My pathology report gave me a breakdown on what was found in my breast tissue that was removed when I had the mastectomy.

Prosthesis—an artificial device used to augment or replace an impaired or missing body part.

Fact: In April 2014, I was fitted for three mastectomy bras and a breast prosthesis. I was amazed at how realistic the prosthesis was! Wearing the prosthesis gives me a sense of balance (no pun intended, or was it?). It also gives me confidence that I don't have when I'm not wearing it. It is a temporary fix until I have my reconstruction surgery in the spring of 2015.

R

Radiation oncologist—a doctor who specializes in overseeing the use of radiation therapy as a treatment method for patients with cancer.

Fact: I first met my radiation oncologist in June 2014 for a consultation. My doctor had explained that I needed thirty treatments of radiation therapy.

Reconstructive surgery—type of surgery performed to replace the breast and the skin of a breast that was previously removed with the goal of restoring symmetry between the two breasts.

Fact: My skin has to heal for six months after my last radiation treatment. My last radiation treatment was September 10, 2014.

Remission—refers to the period when a disease appears to be inactive. A complete remission indicates no sign of the disease. Partial remission indicates that there is a significant decrease in the number of decreased cells and a few symptoms remain.

Fact: I have been in remission since July 10, 2014! I had a CT scan done on July 7, 2014, and the results came back: *no cancer cells in my body!* God is good—all the time! ☺

T

Tamoxifen—an antiestrogen commonly used in hormone treatment therapy due to its ability to block the actions of the female hormone, estrogen.

Fact: I started taking tamoxifen on September 29, 2014. May 2014 to September 29, 2014, I had a nice, long break from my menstrual cycle. It returned after taking one 20 mg pill of tamoxifen! What happened was that my last round of chemotherapy with Taxol had put my body in a premenopausal state. I have to take tamoxifen daily for the next five years!

TRAM flap—surgical procedure that used the transverse rectus abdominis myocutaneous (TRAM) flap to carry lower abdominal fat muscle and skin to the breast in reconstructive surgery as an alternative to a prosthesis.

Fact: My reconstruction surgery will be done using the TRAM flap procedure. It is a transport surgery, which means the surgeons have to make sure that tissues and blood flow are correct. It's an extensive eight-to-ten hour surgery with a minimum of four days in the hospital.

U

Ultrasound examination—a noninvasive painless imaging method that uses high-frequency sound waves to produce fairly precise images of the body's organs and structures. It is used by doctors to diagnose and treat a variety of medical conditions.

Fact: My ultrasound I had performed in December 2013 revealed unsettling images. The doctor decided to do the mammogram and core-needle biopsy.

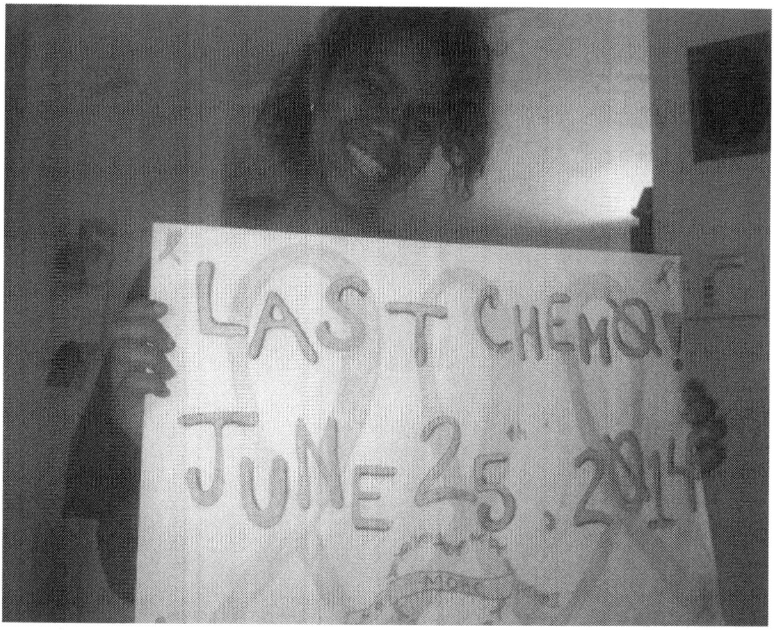
LAST CHEMO!
JUNE 25th, 2014
MORE

Anastasia
Bingham

1/7/2014

8

I've Got Some Mail! I'm Sharing Some Cards and Letters from My Family, Friends, and Coworkers!

Dearest Nicole,

Your presence lights up the whole school. I enjoy seeing you work so hard in your job. You have such a sweetness about you. You are very kind and patient.

You put a smile on my face. I am so inspired by your courage and optimism. I wish the very best for you and your family. Your boys are beautiful. Thank you for blessing us all.
Love, Emily Dalling & Family

1-28-14

Nikki —

People who know
where your journey started
are happy to see
how far you've come,
how strong and determined
you still are.

XOXOXO

May God continue to heal
and strengthen your body, mind
& your quintessential spirit!
With all our love
Mom & Wil

Love and Hugs
To: Annie
Marcos
&
Caesar

Hoping you're blessed
by angels above,
surrounded by smiles,
and encouraged by love...

Nikki

Hoping it helps
your recovery, too,
to know many friends
will be thinking of you!

My daily petition to
God for you:
 May god heal you,
  body and soul.
 May your pain cease,
 May your strength increase
 May your fears be released,
 And may blessings, love + joy
  surround you. ~ amen

My love + friendship always,
 Linda

*Every day, may you
learn more and more
about your own strength,
lean more and more
upon your remarkable courage.*

Nikki,
Every update from you is inspiring! To see that you can overcome Anything handed to you is an example of how resiliant we all should be!

Love You!

Jayce

2/7/14

Nikki ☺
I'm thinking feel-betterish thoughts
just as fast as I can.

Love & Hugs to
Annie, Marcos, & Caesar

"If ever there is tomorrow when
we're not together there is
something you must always
remember. You are braver than
you believe, stronger than you
seem and smarter than you
think. But the most important
thing is, even if we're apart I'll
always be with you" - Winnie
the Pooh ☺   Love Always
                Mom & Wil

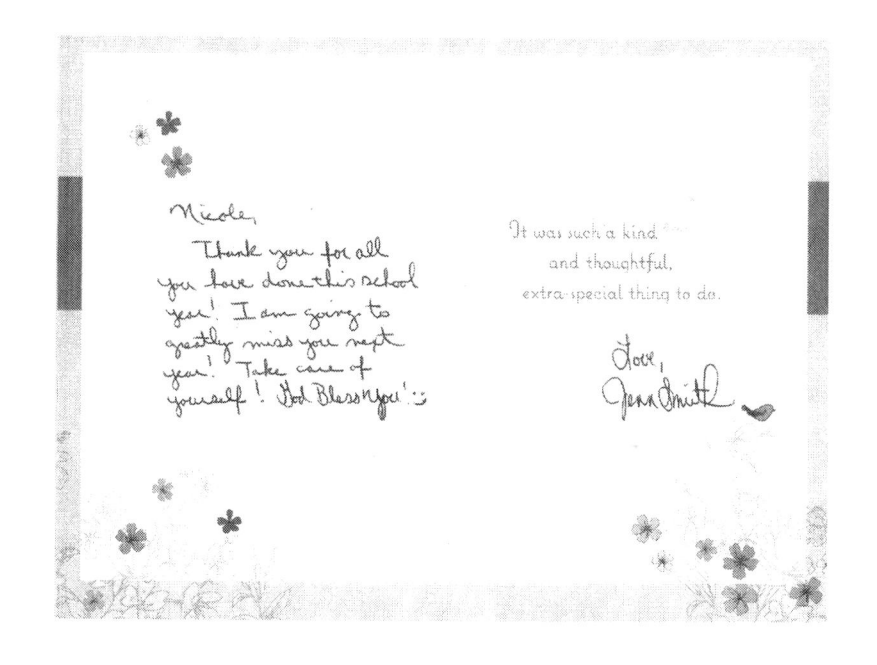

> Nicole,
> Thank you for all you have done this school year! I am going to greatly miss you next year! Take care of yourself! God Bless You! :)
>
> It was such a kind and thoughtful, extra special thing to do.
>
> Love,
> Jenn Smith

> Nicole,
> You are dealing with so much and handling things so well. You are an inspiration to everyone. I am praying for you and Janelle, cheering you on. Love you much.
>
> — Danielle
>
> You mean so much to so many who hope you feel better each day.
>
> Love, Daliah

Dear Nikki,
I just wanted to let you know I was thinking about you. Please know you have been in my thoughts & prayers ever since we heard the news. I will be thinking about you & say extra prayers on the 28th. You're a strong woman & I know you'll kick cancer's butt! Prayers coming your way for a quick & easy recovery. Take it easy as much as possible. I enclosed some quotes that I really like & think you will too.

Warm thoughts and good wishes are with you. Hope you're feeling much better very soon.

Lots of prayers, love and positive thoughts coming your way

Love,
Cindy
& Family

Just wanted to say Hi :) you are always in our thoughts + prayers. Hope you are feeling a little better. Say hi to your beautiful kids for me. Keep Smiling :)

"Feed your faith and your fears will starve to death" — Unknown

...BUT YOU'RE TOUGHER!

Love,
Cindy

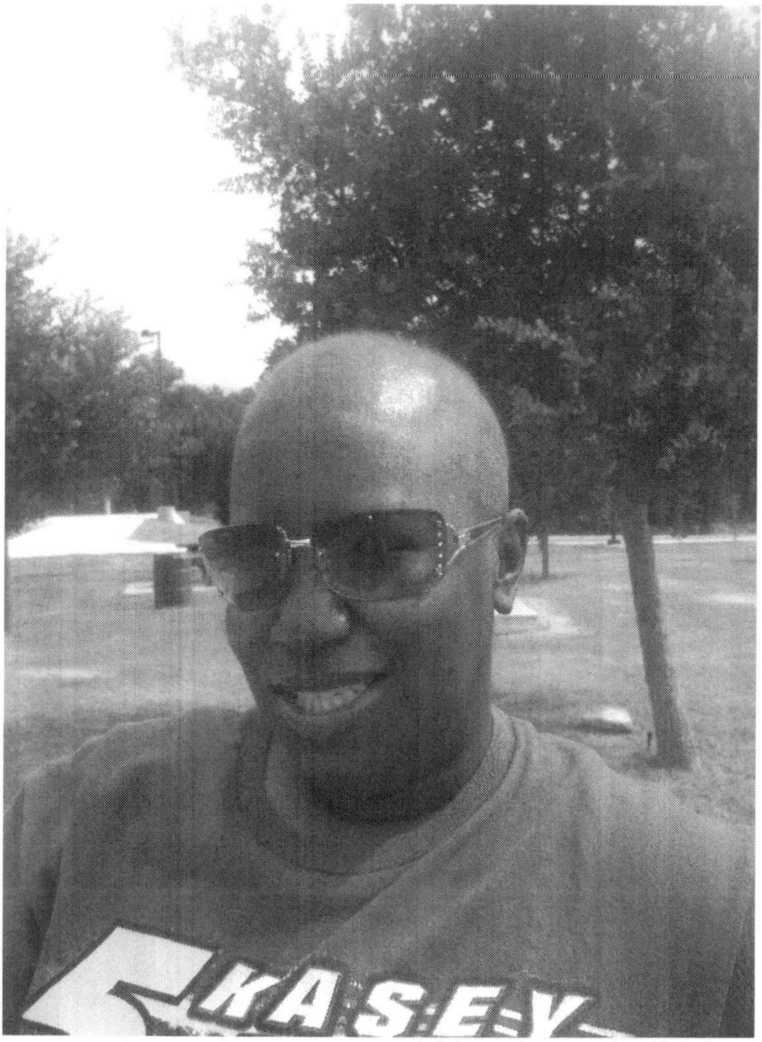
K-A-S-E-Y

9

Raising Breast Cancer Awareness Every Day! Telling My Story to Encourage Women (Especially Women Under Forty) to Get Yearly Mammograms!

The purpose of my book, *I Fought Like a Girl, and I Won!*, is to share my story. Every breast cancer story is different and unique.

I cannot say enough times how important it is as a woman to do monthly self-exams! Don't wait to get a detected lump examined by your doctor. "It's better to be safe than sorry" is an understatement; more importantly, if you have a family history of breast cancer, you need to be checked. If you're under forty and you're told that you're too young to get a mammogram, then you need and have the right to get a second opinion! Don't take no for an answer when it comes to your health. It's 2015 now, and women are being diagnosed with breast cancer in their twenties!

We've all heard it before: early detection is best, and that is the truth! I was fortunate that I found the lump early before it spread to my other organs. Women who are diagnosed early with breast cancer have about a 95 percent survival rate. Life really is too short, so don't gamble with your chances of surviving if you find a lump. A breast cancer scare is very scary, but for most women, a lump is benign.

I have been in remission since July 10, 2014, which coincidentally is my diagnosis date flipped January 7, 2014! I had a CAT scan performed on July 3 to verify that there were no more cancer cells in my body!

Peace of mind is what I wanted and needed after the ordeal I have been through! I continue to see my oncologist and my radiologist physicians every three months for checkups and labs. I am overjoyed to have been blessed with a second chance in life! There are too many other women who have lost their battles with breast cancer. I want to raise breast cancer awareness every day, not just in the month of October. I inspired myself and had the self-motivation to write this book and tell my story to help spread breast cancer awareness worldwide!

Thank you for purchasing and reading my story!

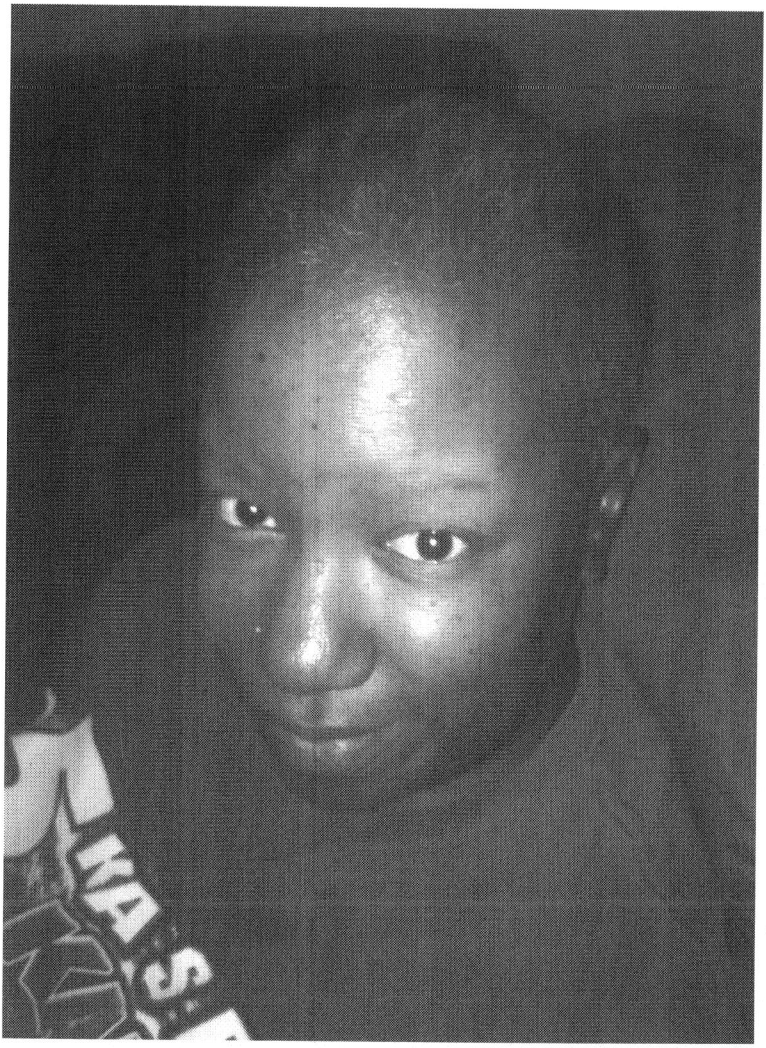

10

Eye of the Tiger! (My Facebook Diary My Mother Created for Me)

CERTIFICATE OF COMPLETION

PRESENTED TO

Nicole Dorman

for completing the prescribed course of Radiation Therapy with the highest degree of Courage, Determination and Good Nature. We appreciate the confidence placed in us and the opportunity to serve you!

S&W

Given this 10th day of September 2014

Jason, Kirst, Adrian
Therapist

Dr. Ord
Physician

Benny, RN
Therapist

LINDA M. KERR

TOBYHANNA, PENNSYLVANIA

29 JUL 14

Dear Ma'am:

I write this letter of reference on behalf of Ms. Nicole Dorman, or Nikki, as she is known to me. I have the incredible honor of knowing Nikki for almost 20 years now. Her Mother and Stepfather were stationed at Tobyhanna Army Depot, where I worked in youth programming. Over the years, I have watched Nikki grow and become a beautiful woman and loving mother. Her life's journey has not been traveled without many challenges. She is a single parent, raising three beautiful, intelligent and compassionate children. Nikki is a United States Army Veteran. She is currently employed by a school district; however it is a part-time job. Her income is very limited and she does not receive support from two of the children's Father.

Most recently, as a matter of fact one week before her birthday in January (2014), Nikki was diagnosed with breast cancer. That is a scary diagnosis for anyone, but to get that diagnosis and know that you are the sole provider for three minor children must have been all the more devastating. Nikki had a mastectomy and then endured four months of chemotherapy. All the while smiling, maintaining a positive attitude and taking care of her three beautiful children; making sure their needs were met and fighting for her life. As of today, Nikki will undergo six weeks of radiation treatment: every day for six weeks! She continues to be determined to beat cancer and win this battle.

Never once have I heard Nikki say, "Why me" or "I can't do this." Her determination, faith in God and commitment to her children are what keep her going and keep her saying, "I will beat this," "I am a survivor!" She quite frankly is an amazing woman: one that I revere and admire beyond words. We all know that nothing in life is guaranteed, but I can say with absolute guarantee, I have never met anyone in my lifetime with more determination than Nicole Dorman: and while it may sound cliché, Nikki truly exemplifies the lyrics of The Eye of the Tiger. She is determined to rise above. She is a survivor and I know that with your help, she can continue to rise above and make a difference in the lives of all who have the honor of knowing her.

Thank you for considering Nikki as a recipient of assistance from your wonderful organization. Should you have any questions for me regarding this reference, please feel free to contact me at (570) 656-8326.

Respectfully,

Linda M. Kerr

MOUNTAIN VIEW ELEMENTARY SCHOOL

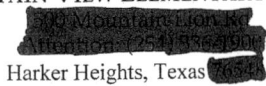

Harker Heights, Texas

Dr. Randy Podhaski 　　Dona Thompson & Grace Ashworth
Principal　　　　　　　　　　Assistant Principals

Every Child, Every Day, Every Where...
No Matter What!

August 14, 2014

To Whom it May Concern,
I am happily writing a letter on behalf of Nikki Dorman.
I have known her for over a year and have known her to be an extremely hard worker. She is always looking for things to do so that she can help out where needed. She does this with such a pleasant attitude and she is always cheerful.

She has had a lot on her plate this past year. She not only is a single parent of three, but then she got the devastating cancer diagnosis. Having breast cancer, going through a mastectomy, 4 months of chemotherapy, and now 6 weeks of radiation, along with being a single parent of 3 children on a limited income of $1,000, didn't stop her from being a great parent and a appreciative employee. She is truly a treasure and deserving of any assistance that you could give her.

If you have any questions, please don't hesitate to call me.

Dona Thompson
Dona Thompson

Memorandum

To: Nicole Dorman
From: Heidi Smotherman, Lead Crossing Guard
C. C. John Dye, Director of Safety
Re: Appreciation Letter

 On Thursday, May 29, the Safety Office sent us an e-mail concerning the "Crossing Guard" at Mountain View, on Wampum and Mt. Lion. Attached is the email.
I just want to say that very few crossing guards get accolades from passing motorists. The fact that you got such an accolade speaks very highly of your attitude, friendliness, and willingness, to be on your corner, in all kinds of weather.

I want to say, Thank you very much, not only for doing a wonderful job, but doing it cheerfully.

You are a credit to the Crossing Guards, Mountain View, and KISD. Keep up the good work.

You are appreciated!!!

Smotherman, Heidi

From:	Dye, John
Sent:	Thursday, May 29, 2014 8:35 AM
To:	Smotherman, Heidi
Subject:	FW: crossing guard

We rarely get good reports.

-----Original Message-----
From: Bradley, Megan
Sent: Thursday, May 29, 2014 8:08 AM
To: Dye, John
Subject: crossing guard

I wanted to take time, before the year ends and I forget, to tell you how friendly one of your crossing guards is. She is at the corner of Wampum and Mountain Lion near Mountain View and Union Grove each morning. She waves to all of the cars as they come through with a big smile on her face (even when it is cold or rainy) and the walkers all seem to chat with her. She helps take the "drab" out of going to school in the morning!

Megan Bradley
Chief Financial Officer
Killeen Independent School District
(254)336-0157

Eye of the Tiger

Jan 7 2014 A week before Nikki's 35th birthday test results of her biopsy show she has a form of breast cancer. We are using this group page for support and to keep family and friends updated on her progress. Nikki is in good spirits and will get more information from her doctors next week. ... And the journey begins. Thank you Jesus for being with us all throughout this journey.

Jan 10 2014 Good Morning Everyone! Words cannot express how blessed, and thankful I am to have such a great support group. I will send updates when I have Appts, etc. I am in good spirits and feeling GREAT today!!

Jan 11 2014 Hi Family and Friends,

The latest update is: since I did not hear from the oncologist I called the department and asked when my first appointment is.... Jan 14, @ 2pm. I was told it is a Q&A appointment and information on what's going to happen from here on out!

I have just created my own campaign page titled Support Nikki's Fight.... I have more details about the type of breast cancer I have. In addition I'm trying to raise money to help pay bills. I read that any type of cancer is an expensive illness. Please encourage your FB friends and family to check it out. You can find my campaign page on FundRazr.com, and do a search for Nicole Dorman my pic is there. Donations can be made by PayPal. I plan to donate some of my proceeds to Saint Jude's Children's Hospital. Have a good weekend everyone and I Love You all for your prayers!

Jan 11 2014 Help Support Nikki's Fight With Breast Cancer!

Hi Everyone,

I am Nicole Dorman, 34, and will be 35 January 15, 2014. I had a core needle breast biopsy on Jan 2, 2014. I received a phone call January 7, 2014 in the afternoon, the results were positive and I was diagnosed with Invasive Ductal Carcinoma. It's a form of breast cancer that can spread throughout my body. It normally affects men and women who are over 45! **On January 2, 2014 I had a right mastectomy,** I am off work until March 3, 2014 to heal and have follow up appointments with my surgeon, and oncologist. I am a single mom to 3 kids ages 6, 8, and 14. I am their sole provider and I cannot let this cancer defeat me! On February 7, 2014 my pathology report stated that I am at Stage 2b. I work part-time for a Texas School as a crossing guard, my job is physical but I love it! My monthly income is $1,100 barely enough to pay rent, utilities, phone bill, and other expenses that arise. I don't have a car, but I get to work to be able to provide for my kids. I am going to be treated at a Texas VA Hospital because I am a Army Veteran. My medical is being taken care but I do have to pay for any prescriptions. I am asking everyone that can to please donate any amout you can to help me and my young children. Your contributions will be greatly appreciate and used towards my monthly bills, getting to my appointments, and prescriptions! I plan to donate a portion of my donations to St. Jude's Children's Research Hospital! Thank-you and God Bless!

Jan 13 2014   Happy Monday Everyone! Hope you all had a great weekend! My weekend was great. Anastazija, Marcos, and Caesar stayed at a friend's house Saturday. I went and did some grocery shopping at HEB, went to Walmart, and had dinner at Applebee's! Sunday was more of a relaxed day where I ironed my clothes, and the boys' clothes for this week. I was going to wait until Tuesday night but I didn't want to overload them with information. Annie took the news the hardest, and Caesar is too young to understand what's going on. I assured them that my illness is not there fault, and that I love them very much!

Jan 13 2014   The ball is moving........ I had my blood draws and had to give a U sample at 7am. Now I am at my primary physician waiting to see Dr. Lopez, who is a female so it makes it easier to talk to another women. I received a phone from VA appointments to tell me I have a surgery consult on Friday at 11am. I will write more after my appt at 9:30am.

Jan 14 2014   Hi Everyone! Here is the latest update: I met with my oncologist Dr.Dodlapati (female). She allowed me to look over my biopsy and ultrasound results while she translated what everything meant. At this time she doesn't know what stage I'm at because a lymph **node has to be taken out during surgery and tested. The mass is 2.5cmx2cm (over 1inch long** and wide) I am at grade 1 which is good, meaning it doesn't look like the cancer cells have spread beyond my right breast. I do have a lot calcification (cancer cells that are old but not invasive). Dr. D says that my short term plan is surgery lumpectomy followed by radiation, or mastectomy. I will find out more about that when I meet with the surgeon Friday. Long term plan is pills or chemo. As for now I have no limitations, and no special diet. I already eat healthy regularly and limit my sweets and fats! Dr. D ordered a CAT scan and a BRCA1, and BRCA2. Those are generic tests to see if I carry a gene for hereditary breast cancer. It is a concern because I'm 34 and my grandma (RIP) died at 48 from breast cancer.

January 15 Nikki's 35th Birthday

Jan 18 2014   Happy Saturday to everyone! I had my consultation with my surgeon yesterday. Surgery will be on Tuesday January 28. The surgeon recommended for me to have a mastectomy with delayed reconstruction. It's an overnight stay at the VA hospital with a minimum of 2 weeks for recovery. I have a few appointments to go to before the 28th that includes an EKG, bone scan , and some more labs.

Jan 23 2014   Good Morning Everyone! I am at the VA for a bone scan appointment. I got the radioactive material injection at 9:15am central time and I have to wait 3 hours before I have the pictures taken. This is my first bone scan, so I was explaining briefly the process to anyone who never had it done. I also had more blood drawn for the BRCA test (genetic testing done see if I'm a carrier for breast cancer gene). Results come in 2-4 weeks, and my oncologist will tell me the results. I am in good spirits today and am trying to remain calm these next few days!!!

Have a blessed day!

Jan 28 2014 ***Photo Posted*** **(pam)** Nikki's surgery went well and right mastectomy was performed as scheduled. Thank you all for your continued prayers for Nikki's full recovery. I talked to Nikki a few minutes ago and she sounded good She will have an overnight stay at the VA Hospital and go home tomorrow. Thank you for your continued prayers for my little girl.

Jan 28 2014 Prayer is very powerful!!! I have God to thank for having a successful surgery and I pray for a speedy recovery. God bless all of my family and friends, and co-workers for all of their prayers and support!!!!!!!

Jan 29 2014 Good Morning To My FTB (fighting the battle) friends and family! I am being discharged this morning! I just talked to a RN who was able to answer some of my questions. The doctors said I don't need a home health nurse because I don't have bandages, I have ALOT of stitches covered with surgical glue. I have been instructed on how to empty out my JP drains and measure the liquid. The drains will stay in 1-2 weeks. I had two ladies who work in the X-ray department come visit me an hour ago. One lady assisted the radiologist technician on Jan 2, 2014 when my biopsy was done, and the other lady did my cat scan last Thursday. Anyways, they asked me if I wanted crackers or cookies to snack on, I said sure and that the graham crackers were good. They came back with a plastic bag full of 2 20 oz sprites, chips ahoy cookies, big bag of Cheetos and some crackers from the cafeteria! It was a nice surprise!

Jan 30 2014 Hi Everyone! I'm just waking up from a nap! I got up early with the kids and signed notebooks and looked at schoolwork. I took my meds and ate a light breakfast with juice. VA did call to check up on me. Everyone, (and I know you all are too) is amazed at how well I am doing and moving around! It definitely will take some time to adjust to my new look!!! GOD IS GOOD ALL THE TIME, and my appearance does not define who I am. My breast is gone but I still have my smile, and am full of life!

Jan 31 2014 Hello everyone! I am happy to announce that I was able to take a bath last night and put on lotion!!!! I feel so much better! Last Sat- Sun I had to bath with pre op soap that left my skin VERY dry. I had to wait 48 hours post surgery to bathe. I am able to raise my right arm all the way up and rotate it as normal which is really good! I brushed my hair too. These are small tasks but I am healing fairly quickly! I know it's the power of prayer, and God **keeping me in his arms! Thank-you all so much. I am still on restrictions to lifting no more** than 10 pounds with my right arm. The JP drains are a pain but they help get rid of excess fluids. I have to be careful how I move around so I don't rip them out. I will have my post surgery check up Feb, 12.

Feb 19 2014 (pam) I talked to Nikki a little while ago and she's doing fine. She's hoping to have more information soon on her treatment plan re chemo and radiation therapy and she's looking forward to going back to work. She'll update her status later. Thank you all for keeping her in your prayers

Feb 20 2014   Good Morning Everyone,

I saw my oncologist on Tuesday. Latest news is I will have to do a radiation consultation at Scott and White in Killeen because the Temple VA doesn't do that. If radiation is needed I will do that after my chemotherapy is completed. My oncologist is waiting to hear from a doctor with answers on when I would start chemo and for how long (something on my pathology report is questionable) I will have to take 2 pills after chemo for 5-10 years!!!! This is to make sure the cancer doesn't return. On Monday I have to do an EKG on my heart to make sure it's healthy enough for me to have a chemo port implanted if I need it! I can't say this enough THANK-YOU ALL FOR YOUR CONTINUED PRAYERS, SUPPORT, AND LOVE!!!!! Have a great Thursday!

March 14 2014 Hello and good morning everyone! I know it's been a while since I posted on here. I have been doing good, I went back to work March 3. This week I was off for spring break. I'm at the oncologist now. I hope to get answers on what my options are for chemo, and when that starts, how long etc. My oncologist did call me on Tuesday to tell me my result for the BRCA1 test was negative! That is a big relief to know that I am not carrier for the **breast cancer gene! Thank-you Lord for all your blessings and watching over all your children!** Amen!!!!! I will update everyone on what's going on when I am finished my appointments! Have a great day!

March 16 2014   (photo posted of micro haircut ~ preparing for chemo)

I'm feeling great now but will post on here later to let you all know how I'm feeling.

March 16 2014   (pam)   Hi All ~ Nikki's getting ready for chemo and still showing how BIG her Brave is ~ she had her hair cut off yesterday to avoid it falling out in clumps. Locks of Love needed her hair to be 10" in order to donate but it's not that long. She will post more soon. Thanks for all your love and prayers for my little girl. Nikki had a bit of trouble with her phone so I'm posting these gorgeous pictures for her

March 19 2014   (pam)   Nikki had surgery yesterday for the port to be put in her jugular vein to receive her chemo. (Ports are used to deliver chemotherapy to cancer patients who must undergo treatment frequently. Chemotherapy is often toxic, and can damage skin and muscle tissue, and therefore should not be delivered through these tissues. Portacaths provide a solution, delivering drugs quickly and efficiently through the entire body via the circulatory system). She sounded good after the procedure and remains positive. Her first chemotherapy treatment is today and either she or I will post later with how she's doing. Thank you all for keeping those prayers coming her way ... And the journey continues.

March 19 2014   I am at my first chemo appt! I'm receiving A LOT of information about Adriamycin, cyclophosphamide, and neulasta which is a shot I give myself in my stomach or bottom 24 hours after I receive my chemo treatments. I have some more prescriptions to pick up when I'm done. Anxiety pills, nausea pills, pills to help me sleep at night if for some reason I can't fall asleep. I'm learning a lot today! Prior to any chemo medicine being administered I have my port flushed, then have a Nausea IV bag (15 min). 15 mins of saline. Both treatments take 30 mins each to go through my port.

(photo posted) 1st chemo session! You can see where my port is. My chest and neck are still very sore!

April 2 2014   Hi Everyone! I'm at the Temple TX VA Hospital getting my second round of chemo! My oncologist put me on stronger nausea medicine to take. i did loose my appetite a few times. I have not had any other side effects! (Knock on wood) I did loose 1 lb lol so far in 2 weeks. Dr. D recommend me to do more stretching and walking but no strenuous exercises.

April 7 2014   Good Afternoon Everyone! I know it's been a few days since I last posted. My second round of chemo on April 2, was more harder than the first round on March 19th. I am having more side effects than the last time ,but that is expected. I am feeling better today than Friday!

April 14 2014 (photo posted)   Happy Monday everyone! I had the rest of my hair cut off is Saturday. The little bit that I had left was falling out!

My spirits were lifted on Saturday when I received 3 cards in the mail!!!! One was from Mary and Jim Maness friends of my mom and Michael from when we lived at the Tobyhanna Army Depot. The other 2 cards had no return address or signature, but they were stamped from Charleston WV. Thank-you all so much for your cards, continued support, love, and prayers.

April 15 2014   Good Morning! More of my spirits were lifted when I checked my mailbox when I came home from work yesterday. I received a postcard from Julia Lewis, Aunt Cindy, Uncle Richard, Linda and John Kerr (thank-you so much for the WalMart Gift Cards, and your prayer petition!!) Thank-you to Katie, my Mom, Wil, my brother Anthony, and his girlfriend Ticcorra for their cards. Tomorrow I have my 3rd round of chemo. I'm ready to get this round over with, and I pray that I will be feeling better in time for Easter! Have a blessed Day!!!!

April 16 2014   Hump Day! I'm at my 3 rd chemo session right now halfway thru my adriamycin drip! My vitals were all normal. I have lost 7 pounds since I started chemo on 3/19!!!!! I discussed with my oncologist the side effects I been having. The bone pain that I have after taking the 6 mg Nuelasta shot is excruciating!!!!!! However, it means that it Is working.

April 18 2014   My spirits were lifted high this morning when I was delivered royal blue box labeled Treasured Keys To Life. I wanted to thank my anonymous gift giver, and also for the Walmart Gift Card!! May you and your family have a blessed Easter! Much Love, Nikki Dorman

I asked the assistant principal of my school I work at and volunteer at to send an email out to all of the employees with the same message I just posted!

April 18 2014   Good Morning Everyone! May all of you have a Good Friday! Just wanted to let everyone know that my 3rd chemo treatment was successful! My white blood count and hemoglobin levels are both good!!!!! My oncologist put me on 150 mg of Gastro Esophageal reflux pills which works MUCH BETTER than the 4mg nausea medicine! She advised me to take my pain pills prior to self administering my Nuelasta shot to avoid the bone pain I had 2 weeks ago! That worked and am feeling great today! My body temp is 97.1 which is my new normal versus the 98.6 and my bp was 122/72 !

April 22 2014 Thank-you to Michael and Marcia and my cousins Daliah, Danielle and Janelle for your cards that I received yesterday!!!! The cards that I have received help to keep me positive, and focused on my fight!

April 26 2014 I thought this posted yesterday.... But it didn't so I am reposting now. Thank-You to my Mom, Wil, Anthony and Ticorra for my "Box of Love" I received yesterday! The surprise box contained a cute and cuddly chemo bear, a neat pair of cushioned headphones that I can use with my iPhone (I don't like ear buds I don't use the pair that came with my phone), an inspirational book titled "Real Moments" by Barbara DeAngelis, Ph.D.,2 cozy pink pairs of socks, and some other things to brighten my spirits!!!! Thank-you soooooo much!

I hope everyone is having a awesome weekend! I received a beautiful card from my cousin Joyce Harrison..... I would like to post what Joyce wrote because it is worth repeating!

Nikki:

Every update from you is inspiring! To see that you can overcome anything handed to you is an example of how resultant we all should be!

Love you!   Joyce

Love you too cousin!!!!

April 30 2014 Thank-you to Aunt Dawn, Uncle Bill, Billy, Christopher and Thomas for your cards that I received in the mail yesterday!!!!!!!!!!!

I had my 4th treatment today, all went well. I do my last shot of Nuelasta Thursday night. I start my next chemo drug May 14, and its called Taxol, I'm told its not as toxic. If all goes well then my final chemo will be June 25!!!!!!!!!

May 3 2014 Thank-you to Linda and John Kerr! When I arrived home on Friday there was a package waiting on the porch for me! My spirits were uplifted from the "surprise package"!!!!!

May 12 2014 Thank-you to Mr. And Katie Mrs. Saldibar for sending me a Box Of Love on Friday. It was a big surprise to see a Scentsy box on the porch! I am new to Scentsy but I know I will love the pineapple scent, and warmer! !!!!!! I adore the pink camouflage blanket and cozy tote socks. I can start reading the Chicken Soup For the Soul Cancer Book on Wed at my 5th chemo session. Thanks for the other goodies in the box!!!!!

May 14 2014 HUMP DAY! HAPPY WEDNESDAY EVERYONE! I'm at my 5th chemotherapy appointment right now. I just started my Taxol drip. There is a Taxol kit on standby, incase I have an allergic reaction to the new med. I had a Benedryl drip 20 mins ago! I'm just happy that I am finished the first to meds and I'm done with the Nuelasta shot!!!!!

I did have an appointment Tuesday with a mastectomy fitter. She was very helpful in getting me the products I need to help me feel normal again!

May 15 2014 *photo posted*   Sporting my new wig!!!!! I got it yesterday at the Fountain Of Beauty Salon and Spa in Temple TX. American Cancer Society donates wigs to them and other vendors!

May 19 2014   Good Morning! Hope everyone had a great weekend!! I received a call this morning from the Scott & White Oncology Clinic in Killeen. I have a 6/18 appointment for my radiation consultation. I'm not out of the woods yet, but I'm getting a step closer to being CANCER FREE!

May 22 2014   Good Morning Everyone! I want to thank Kim Hawkins in Pipestem WV for mailing me out a box of love!!!!! It was waiting on the porch for me! I love the COOL GEAR insulated mug with option to sip or chug! Lol. Some other items in the box were Juicy Fruit gum, Mambo fruit chews, word search book (love doing these!), Subway gift-card, diary book, THIRTY ONE purple bag (my fave color) Thank -You again to EVERYONE for you support, posting messages on Eye Of The Tiger, viewing messages on Eye Of The Tiger, your cards, PRAYER, LOVE!!!!! THANK- YOU to Mary and Jim for your card I received on Tuesday this week.

Here is YOUR THOUGHT FOR TODAY! This is from an unknown author (maybe you've read it before)

LIVE EACH DAY WITH GRATITUDE

Gratitude is one of life's greatest gifts and is free for the choosing. When we make this choice, we are demonstrating an understanding I'd our free will.

Gratitude is a practice...an exercise in which we train our minds to look at the good things before us each day, no matter what is happening in our lives.

Gratitude is a state of mind we cultivate in ourselves that enables us to understand that often it is our greatest challenges and losses that brings us our greatest lessons.

Gratitude is the place from which we recognize life's compensations that are always before us, so we can enjoy each day with thanksgiving.

May 28 2014   Hi everyone! I just completed my 6th chemo treatment today! 2 more to go! I was prescribed nerve pain med, so when I get the fibromyalgia like pain it should help. My doctor put in a consultation with the plastic surgeon so I should be receiving a call for that appointment soon and go from there! All my vitals and labs looked good, Praise The Lord!

Eye of the Tiger ~

Thank-You shout out to Michelle Meaney-Demarsh who contacted Jersey Shore Huggers. This company sent me two crocheted hats. One is pink and one is navy blue!

June 4 2014   I didn't have any chemo today, but I am down to my last 2 treatments!!!!! June 11th and 25th!!! My radiation consultation is on June 18th, and I have a plastic surgeon consultation on June 20th! I am praying that I don't need radiation but if I do, hopefully it won't be a lengthy treatment!!!!

Good Morning everyone! I hope everyone's Wednesday is going GREAT. I just wanted to post to let everyone know that I am feeling great!

On Tuesday I received a box of love from my cousin Daliah Jones Holmes and her daughters' Danielle and Janelle! The box contained a beautiful wicker storage box that contained a subway gift card, jolly ranchers, peppermints, 2 foldable water bottles (pretty neat!) a inspirational card, and a blistek.

June 6 2014   Hello Everyone, I hope you all had a great Friday! I received a box of love from Michelle-Demarsh on Thursday!!!! The box contained an orange Calvin Klein scarf, a bottle if massaging lotion, and pajamas In a bottle! It's relaxation lotion that has lavender and chamomile! Other surprise goodies included a bar of acai berry soap..........and........drum roll please....

Sorry for the delay, my phone is acting up...

I love this awesome personalized Thirty-One bag Michelle!!!!!! Thank-You so much!!!!!

June 8 2014   Another Fantastic, thoughtful, spirit lifting, box of love arrived on Saturday from Linda and John Kerr!!!!!! In the box I found a cute pink Beanie Baby named Promise. She is wearing the pink ribbon!!!! A cd called HOPE- songs to celebrate life, Hallmark Keepsake Ornament - Snowman Angel wearing a pink knitted scarf on the bottom of the snowman it says: Surrounded By Caring. Notepad and pen, N stationary that is pink, a musical card that is very nice! Saving the best for last........ I received another ornament that is a Waterford Crystal, absolutely beautiful! Thank-you sooooooooo much Linda and John!!!!!

June 10 2014 (photo posted)   It's the end of the school year ~ Let the summer begin

June 11 2014   GM everyone! I want to thank Amanda and Antwoine Robinson for their card, and Target GC! Also thank you to Mike Kulikowski Jr. for your note!

June 16 2014   Hi Everyone,

I received a surprise box of love from Julia Lewis on Saturday! The box included: A Nivea Kiss

Collection 3 lip butters, and 2 lip care sticks with SPF. Raspberry, Cranberry, and, Blueberry Tea, and a honey bear. Two books.....1) Be Unique- Peanuts Wisdom to Carry You Through 2) Life Songs- Giving Voice To The Spirit Within, and a nice purple fashion scarf! Thank-you again Julia!

Wishing everyone a Blessed Week! I will be updating everyone after my appts on Wednesday, and Friday this week!!

June 18 2014   Good Evening Everyone! Today I had my radiation consultation. The doctor told me because of the results of my pathology report and my age, I must undergo radiation. It's not the end of the world, but that's not what I wanted to hear! I will start radiation the end of July, for 30 treatments. So I will be going Mon-Fri for 6 weeks. This radiation therapy will postpone my reconstruction surgery for 6 months after the last treatment.

June 21 2014   Hi Everyone! Just an update about my appointment with the plastic surgeon. Without going into too much details, I can choose between 2 different surgeries. 1 being a simpler procedure than the other

And less healing time. I will be praying on everything. I have a follow up appt in Dec with the doctor and to make my final decision!!! Right now I'm just excited and prepared for my final chemo on Wed June 25th!!!!!! One step at a time, another chapter completed in my book of life!

Have a great weekend!

June 25 201   *Several photos posted* Hi Everyone! Happy Hump Day!!

I'm at my final chemo appointment! I am blessed to have conquered 8 rounds of chemo every 2 weeks! This is another milestone in my life! I couldn't have done it alone. Today is a celebration of new life, dreams, and the power of prayer!!!! Can I get a Amen?!

I will post the pics. My Aunt Dee-Dee brought me here today! BTW my daughter Anastazija made me a poster!

June 26 2014   A big Thank-You to Ameisha Jo Boone for mailing me a Box Of Love! I received your package on Saturday. The package contained Mascara, 2 nail polishes, candy, pic frames, a BEAUTIFUL Willow Tree Loving Angel, and Bath and Body Works lotion, spray, and bath gel! Thank You again Amisha!

July 3 2014 (photos posted)   Wishing Everyone a Happy and SAFE 4th of July! Here are two pics of my blonde hair coming in, it's very light!!!!! . I'm looking forward to seeing how much it grows in weekly!

July 10 2014   Happy Thursday Everyone!

I am over joyous, to report that I had a CAT Scan done today at the VA. My oncologist called me at 11:46am to let me know that everything looked good, and that there are NO CANCER

CELLS in my body! It has been said so many times before, and is worth repeating! God Is Good, All The Time!

When i had my final chemo on June 25th I requested to have the CAT SCAN done so I could have piece of mind. I still have to go through radiation treatments for 6 weeks starting the end of July. My new hair continues to grow in, I will be posting weekly pictures, for everyone to see my hair growth progress!

I received a box of love from Cheryl Davis July 9th! Her package contained, a word search book and pencil, 3 fruit flavored soaps, Thomas Kinkade Gospel Songs CD! Thank-You so much Cheryl!

Before I post this for today.......

I encourage all my female friends and family no matter what your age is......If you detect a lump,don't delay please get it checked out! 40 is not the age to start getting mammograms, that is not the case anymore. Sadly enough females are being diagnosed with BC as young as in their teens! Also BC is not as common in men, but men can get it too, so remember "When in doubt, get that lump checked out!"

July 16 2014 (photo posted) Good Afternoon everyone, Today I had my radiation CT simulation. I will begin radiation daily on July 30th for 6 weeks. My radiologist Dr. have me an information packet with possible short and long time side effects. Here is my hair pic for this week!

July 22 2014 I would like to send a HUGE thank-you to Linda and John Kerr for sending another FANTASTIC BOX OF LOVE for my Children. I was completely blown away when I opened the box and seen three personalized bags for school, and school supplies. Anastazija, Marcos, and Caesar will go back to school with these unique initialed Thirty-One bags!!!!!!

P.S. I will definitely be wearing the breast cancer ribbon lanyard, and Thirty-One I.D. Card holder when I return back to work August 25th!!!!

July 24 2014 (photo posted) Here is my artistic daughter Anastazija, showing her special Spider-Man drawing for Danny Nickerson. He is the little boy who turns 6 tomorrow. Danny has an inoperative brain tumor, and wanted nothing but cards for his 6th birthday. We are mailing out his birthday drawing today!

July 31 2014 Hello Everyone! Throwback Thursday!!!!!!

My first radiation appointment went well yesterday. I had to lay on a table. The area being treated was drawn on with a sharpie. I have a few clear stickers on me that I have to leave on for the duration of the treatment period of 6 weeks. I had to get x-rays done of the areas I'm having radiation on. The areas being treated are on the right side of my neck, collar bone, and mastectomy site. I have to lay on the table with my arms above my head holding onto a bar. A gel material is placed on my chest and then the radiologist technologist leave the room. A machine with a red beam goes over the site being treated for 10 mins. I was there for 45 mins yesterday because of the set up, and x-rays. My radiologist oncologist told me that some side effects I may get are fatigue, darkening of the skin, and peeling of the skin (over time). Of course there are other side effects that other people have experienced like blisters, but I pray that I will not have that!!!!! I have to use a mild soap and lotions on the treatment sites, I will have radiation daily for 6 weeks.

Have a great day everyone!

July 30 2014 (photo posted)   This is my selfie for today July 30, 2014.

August 15 2014 (photo posted) Hi Everyone!!!!!   I am doing great, and feeling good! Radiation is going good, I have had 13 treatments so far, 17 more to go! I feel a little fatigue but its not as bad as chemo was. Radiation is a walk in the park in comparison! "Hair" are my shots for this week! LOL

September 11 2014   Hello everyone! I know it's been awhile since I've written on here, I apologize. Yesterday I finished my radiation treatments! I have had 30 treatments total. On the flip side I do have a lot of painful radiation burns, and swelling. My skin started peeling last Friday. My doctor said I should be healed in 2-4 weeks. I have been briefed on skin care, and am taking pain medicine at night!

Another chapter of my breast cancer journey is completed! God is good!!!!!

September 25 2014   Hi everyone! I hope everyone is doing good and that your all in good health! It's been a min since I posted a selfie. Last one I posted of my hair growth process was around 5 weeks ago. So here is a pic of me I took today! I had an appt at the VA on Monday with my oncologist. I last seen her on 6-25-14 for my last chemo. She said that I looked good, labs were good, and she prescribed my prescription for Tamoxifen. That's the pill I have to take daily for 5 years!!!!! It's whatever it takes to stay healthy right! After all taking a pill is nothing compared to conquering surgery, chemo, and radiation!!!!!!!

I had a follow up with my radiologist yesterday for my 2 week follow up. She said my new skin growth looks good. I'm still peeling a little bit, but i am not in pain like I was.

October 6 2014 (photo posted) TO ALL WOMEN WHO ARE BATTLING BREAST CANCER, KEEP FIGHTING THE FIGHT! THE CANCER FIGHT IS A CHALLENGE, BUT WITH HELP, SUPPORT, AND LOVE FROM FRIENDS AND FAMILY THE FIGHT CAN BE WON! I CAN TESTIFY TO THAT! THANK-YOU TO EVERYONE WHO HAS SUPPORTED ME THROUGH MY JOURNEY

" Nikki Won The Fight "

October 12 2014 (photo posted) Selfie with pink ribbbon on cheek

October 27 2014 (newspaper photo posted)   I wanted to share this newspaper article with everyone. I took a pic of it so I hope that you can read most of the article!

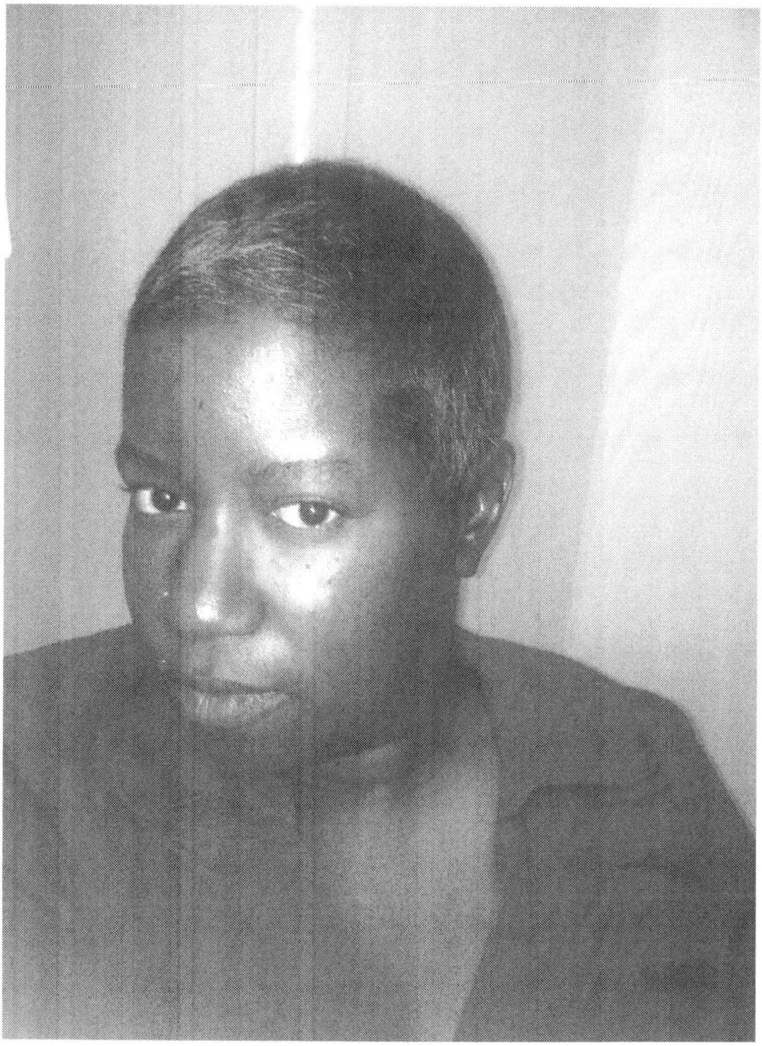

Anastazeja Bingham
11/26/2014

11

Breast Cancer Resources

A breast cancer diagnosis is very stressful and a hard pill to swallow! There are mixed emotions from everyone you tell the news to, and you will feel overwhelmed like there is nowhere to go for help. There is help out there for financial, cleaning, prescriptions, and other expenses; you just have to know where to find it. The Internet is a wealth of knowledge and a very powerful tool! This resource guide is to let you know that you're not alone in your journey!

- Academy of Nutrition and Dietetics (www.eatright.org)
- Adjuvant (www.adjuvantonline.com)
- American Cancer Society (www.cancer.org)
- American College of Radiology (www.acr.org)
- American Institute for Cancer Research (www.aicr.org)
- American Medical Association (www.ama-assn.org)

- American Psychosocial Oncology Society (www.apos-society.org/survivors/helpline/helpline.aspx)
- American Society of Plastic Surgeons (www.plasticsurgery.org/reconstructive-proceedures/breast-reconstructions)
- Angel Flight (www.angelflight.com)
- Army of Women (www.armyofwomen.org)
- Breakaway from Cancer (www.breakawayfromcancer.com/breastcancer.org)
- Breast Cancer Freebies (www.breastcancerfreebies.com)
- CancerCare (www.cancercare.org)
- Cancer.Net (www.cancer.net)
- Cancer Support Community (www.cancersupportcommunity.org)
- Cancer Treatment Centers of America (www.cancercenter.com)
- CaringBridge (www.caringbridge.org)
- Cleaning for a Reason (www.cleaningforareason.com)
- Chemo Angels (www.chemoangels.wix.com)
- Dream Foundation (www.dreamfoundation.org)
- Dr. Susan Love Research Foundation (www.dslrf.com)
- Fertile Hope (www.fertilehope.org)
- FORCE (Facing Our Risk of Cancer Empowered) (www.facingourrisk.org)
- Foundation for Women's Cancer (www.foundationforwomenscancer.org)

- Hope for Two... The Pregnant with Cancer Network (www.pregnantwithcancer.org)
- Imerman Angels (www.imermanangels.org)
- Inflammatory Breast Cancer (IBC) Research Foundation (www.ibcresearch.org)
- LIVESTRONG Foundation (www.livestrong.org)
- Living Beyond Breast Cancer (www.lbbc.org)
- Locks of Love (www.locksoflove.org)
- Look Good... Feel Better (www.lookgoodfeelbetter.org)
- MD Anderson Cancer Center (www.mdanderson.org)
- Medscape (www.medscape.com)
- Metastatic Breast Cancer Network (MBCN) (www.mbcn.org)
- National Breast Cancer Coalition (www.breastcancerdeadline2020.org)
- National Cancer Institute (www.cancer.gov)
- National Center for Complementary and Alternative Medicine (NCCAM) (www.nccam.nih.gov)
- National Coalition for Cancer Survivorship (NCCS) (www.canceradvocacy.org)
- National Comprehensive Cancer Network (www.nccn.com)
- National Hospice and Palliative Care Organization (www.nhpco.org)
- National Institutes of Health (www.nih.gov)

- National Lymphedema Network (NLN) (www.lymphnet.org)
- National Society of Genetic Counselors (www.nsgc.org)
- NC1-Designated Cancer Centers (www.cancer.gov/researchfunding/extramural/cancercenters/find-a-cancer-center)
- Office of Cancer Complementary and Alternative Medicine (OCCAM) (www.cam.center.gov)
- Prevent Cancer Foundation (www.preventcancer.org)
- Reach to Recovery Program (www.cancer.org/treatment/supportprogramservices/reach-to-recovery)
- Sisters Network, Inc. (www.sistersnetworkinc.org)
- Stand Up To Cancer (SU2C) (www.standup2cancer.org)
- Susan G. Komen Breast Cancer Foundation (ww5.komen.org)
- Triple Negative Breast Cancer (TNBC) Foundation, Inc. (www.tnbcfoundation.org)
- US Food and Drug Administration (www.fda.gov)
- Young Survival Coalition (www.youngsurvival.org)

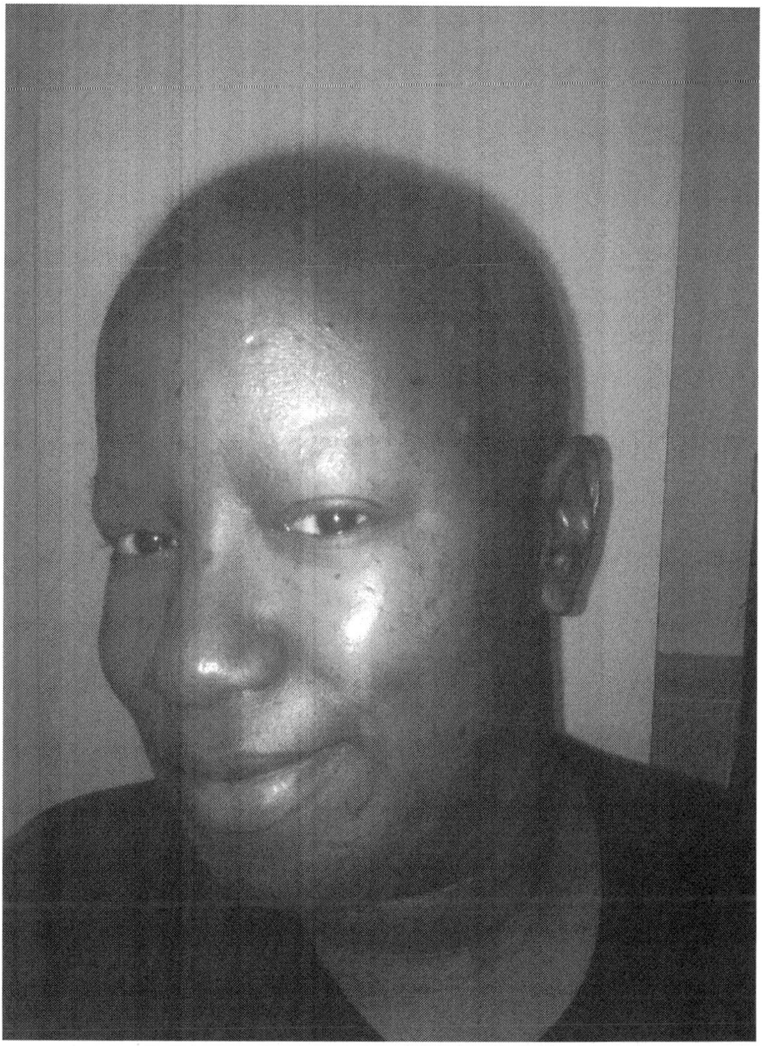

Made in the USA
Lexington, KY
24 May 2015